The Painted Photographs of Melvin Charney

BETWEEN OBSERVATION AND INTERVENTION

EDITED BY GABRIELA RANGEL AND GWENDOLYN OWENS

Published in conjunction with the exhibition *Between Observation and Intervention: The Painted Photographs of Melvin Charney,* on view at the Americas Society Art Gallery from May 1 to July 31, 2008.

The exhibition and publication are produced by Americas Society in collaboration with the Musée national des beaux-arts du Québec.

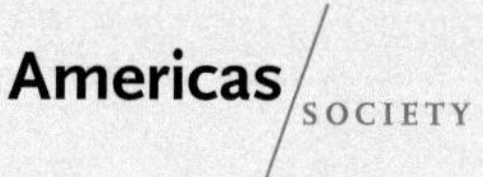

The publication of this book is made possible in part by a grant from the Graham Foundation for Advanced Studies in the Fine Arts.

The Visual Arts Program is supported in part by public funds from the New York City Department of Cultural Affairs

Americas Society gratefully acknowledges the following donors for their generous support of the exhibition: Government of Canada, Consulate General of Canada, New York; Government of Québec, Québec Government Office in New York; Parnassus Foundation, courtesy of Jane and Raphael Bernstein; Power Corporation of Canada; and Rosamond Ivey. The exhibition is also made possible in part with public funds from the New York State Council on the Arts, a State Agency. Additional support has been received from the Nicholas Metivier Gallery, Toronto.

Musée national des beaux-arts du Québec gratefully acknowledges the following donors and partners for their generous support of the exhibition: American Apparel Canada; Gluskin Sheff + Associates Inc.; the Webster Foundation; the Department of Foreign Affairs and International Trade, Canada; Canada Council for the Arts; and anonymous donors. The Musée national des beaux-arts du Québec is a government corporation funded by the Ministère de la Culture, des Communications et de la Condition féminine du Québec.

Melvin Charney would also like to thank the Conseil des arts et des lettres du Québec for its support.

CATALOGUE EDITORS
Gwendolyn Owens
Gabriela Rangel

ASSISTANT EDITOR AND
PUBLICATION COORDINATOR
Isabela Villanueva

COPY EDITOR
Marcie Muscat

CATALOGUE DESIGN
Kate Johnson

Published by Americas Society
680 Park Avenue, New York, NY 10065

Printed in the U.S. by GHP

Publishing © 2009 by Americas Society

Texts © 2009 by the authors

ISBN 978-1-879128-73-6

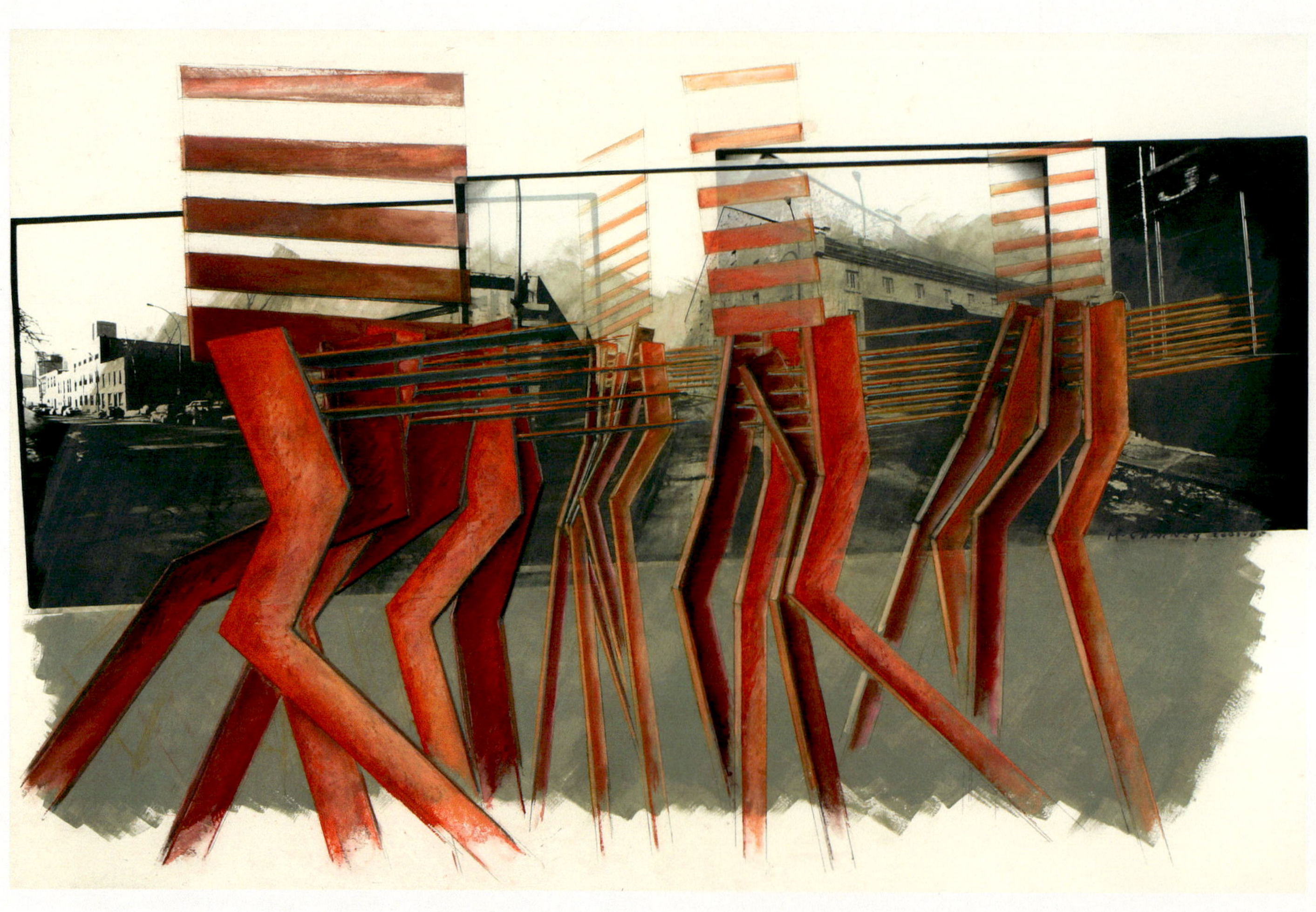

CITIES ON THE RUN... on the edges of industrial belts, 2002–05. Oil pastel and acrylic on a montage of three laser prints of original photographs mounted on board. 101.5 x 152.5 cm. (40 x 60 in.) Rosamund Ivey Collection, Toronto.

Americas Society takes deep pride in presenting the publication *The Painted Photographs of Melvin Charney: Between Observation and Intervention*. It is our hope that, with this book, a large audience in the United States and Canada will take a deeper look at the artist's painted photographs series. The contributors to this volume will incite us to think about new readings of individual building types, the nature of the city, and our complex (and conflicted) relationship to both.

This publication completes a cycle begun in the spring of 2008, when Americas Society presented the exhibition *Between Observation and Intervention: The Painted Photographs of Melvin Charney*, curated by Gwendolyn Owens. Our goal has been the increased recognition and understanding of Melvin Charney's contributions to art, architecture, and the urban environment in the United States. The artist's extensive involvement in this project ensures that the publication reflects his most current thinking about the city and the critical issues he has addressed throughout his career. The publication will enable a broader audience to view and understand the work of this important conceptual artist, and encourage relevant, stimulating, and challenging discussions about the urban fabric in the twenty-first century.

The exhibition at Americas Society was Charney's first solo show in New York since his installation at P.S.1 Contemporary Art Center in 1979. It featured twenty-eight painted photographs and two *CITIES ON THE RUN* sculptures, as well as text and images about Charney's major built projects, including *Les Maisons de la rue Sherbrooke*, destroyed in 1976 by order of the mayor of Montréal.

This publication is an important document of Charney's ideas, reflecting the development of his research over the past forty years and the impact they have had on art, architecture, and thinking about the urban environment. It represents an innovative and timely contribution to the existing body of scholarly work about Melvin Charney.

This project is of special significance to Americas Society because of our hemispheric mission to foster a broader understanding and appreciation of the rich cultural heritage of our neighbors in Latin America, the Caribbean, and Canada. In addition, the Americas Society Visual Arts department has long sought to present exhibitions and publications on artistic practices that deserve greater attention in the United States. *The Painted Photographs of Melvin Charney* continues this pioneering tradition.

I wish to commend Melvin Charney, Gwendolyn Owens, Phyllis Lambert, Cecil Rabinovitch, Fabienne Bilodeau, and the Director and curatorial staff of the Musée national des beaux-arts du Québec; and Gabriela Rangel, Isabela Villanueva, and Mariela Hardy at the Americas Society's Visual Arts department, who all put forth their best efforts for the successful realization of this project.

SUSAN SEGAL
President and CEO, Americas Society

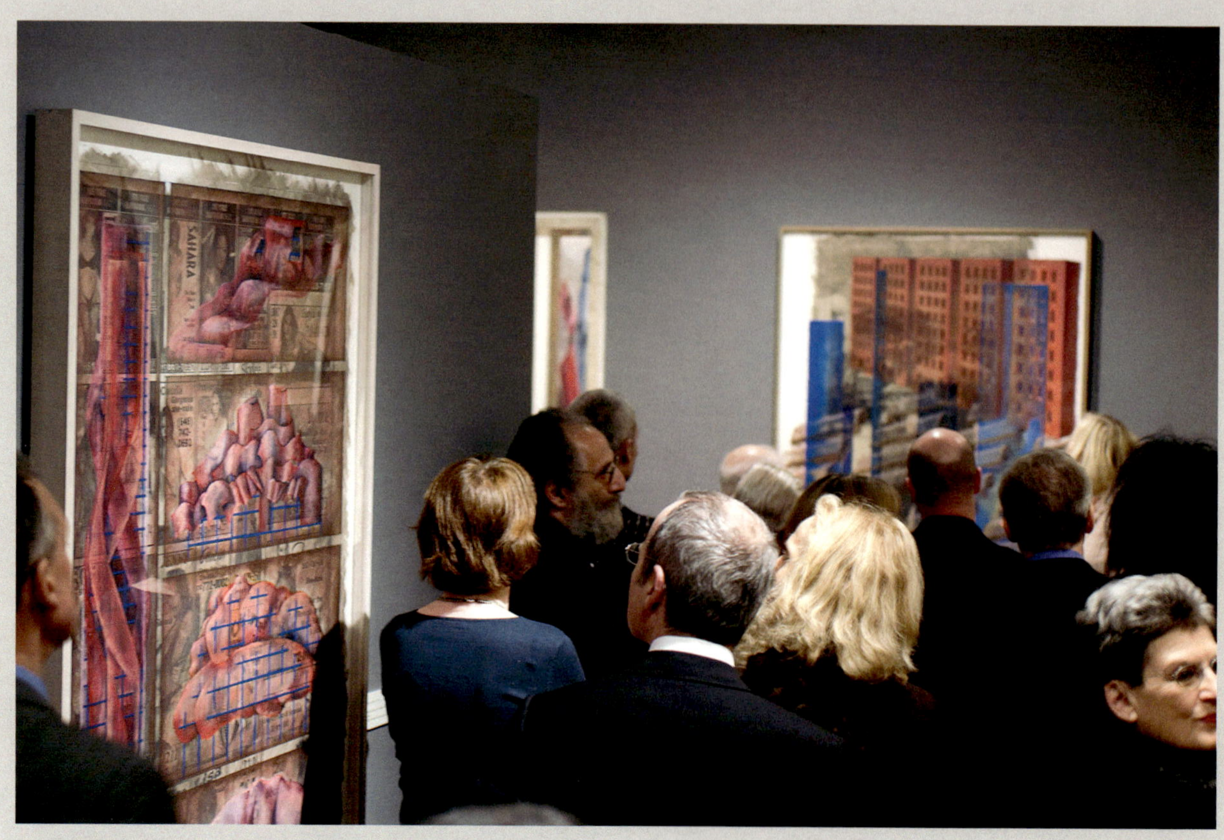

Between Observation and Intervention: The Painted Photographs of Melvin Charney, Americas Society, 2008. Installation view including the following artwork (left to right): *ONE FIT SIZES ALL/3: Blobs on the Grid...* 2002; *FATHER AND SONS...* 1996–97. Photo: Arturo Sanchez.

The work of Melvin Charney provokes numerous thoughtful reflections on the intersection between art and architecture as well as on society and architectural practice.

Between Observation and Intervention: The Painted Photographs of Melvin Charney is the second collaborative project of the Musée national des beaux-arts du Québec and Americas Society. In 1995 we were fortunate to work together on *Visions of Light and Air: Canadian Impressionism, 1885–1920,* an exhibition held both in New York and Québec, which produced a book that is considered to be among the most important publications on the subject. We have every certainty that this publication on Melvin Charney will also be considered an essential reference.

We would like to salute the work of the guest curator of this exhibition, Gwendolyn Owens, and of Gabriela Rangel, Director of Visual Arts at Americas Society, who supervised the project. On our side, we would like to acknowledge the important role of Michel Martin, Curator, and Line Ouellet, Director of Exhibitions, at the Musée national des beaux-arts du Québec.

We would also like to thank our partners in Canada who helped make this exhibition possible: the Canada Council, the Canadian Department of Foreign Affairs and International Trade, as well as the generous donors American Apparel Canada, Gluskin Sheff + Associates, Inc., the Webster Foundation, and anonymous contributors.

Over the years, the Musée national des beaux-arts du Québec has assembled a collection of Melvin Charney's work that is among the finest and most comprehensive in Canada. We are particularly delighted to have recently added two important works shown in this exhibition, *THE AMERICAN CITY: Henry and Friends, Detroit, circa 1970…* and *THE AMERICAN CITY: Ieho Ming & Friends, Manhattan 1989,* to our collection. Through this exhibition and this publication, we are pleased to introduce to a wider American audience the work of this important Canadian artist.

ESTHER TRÉPANIER, PH.D.
Directrice générale du Musée national des beaux-arts du Québec

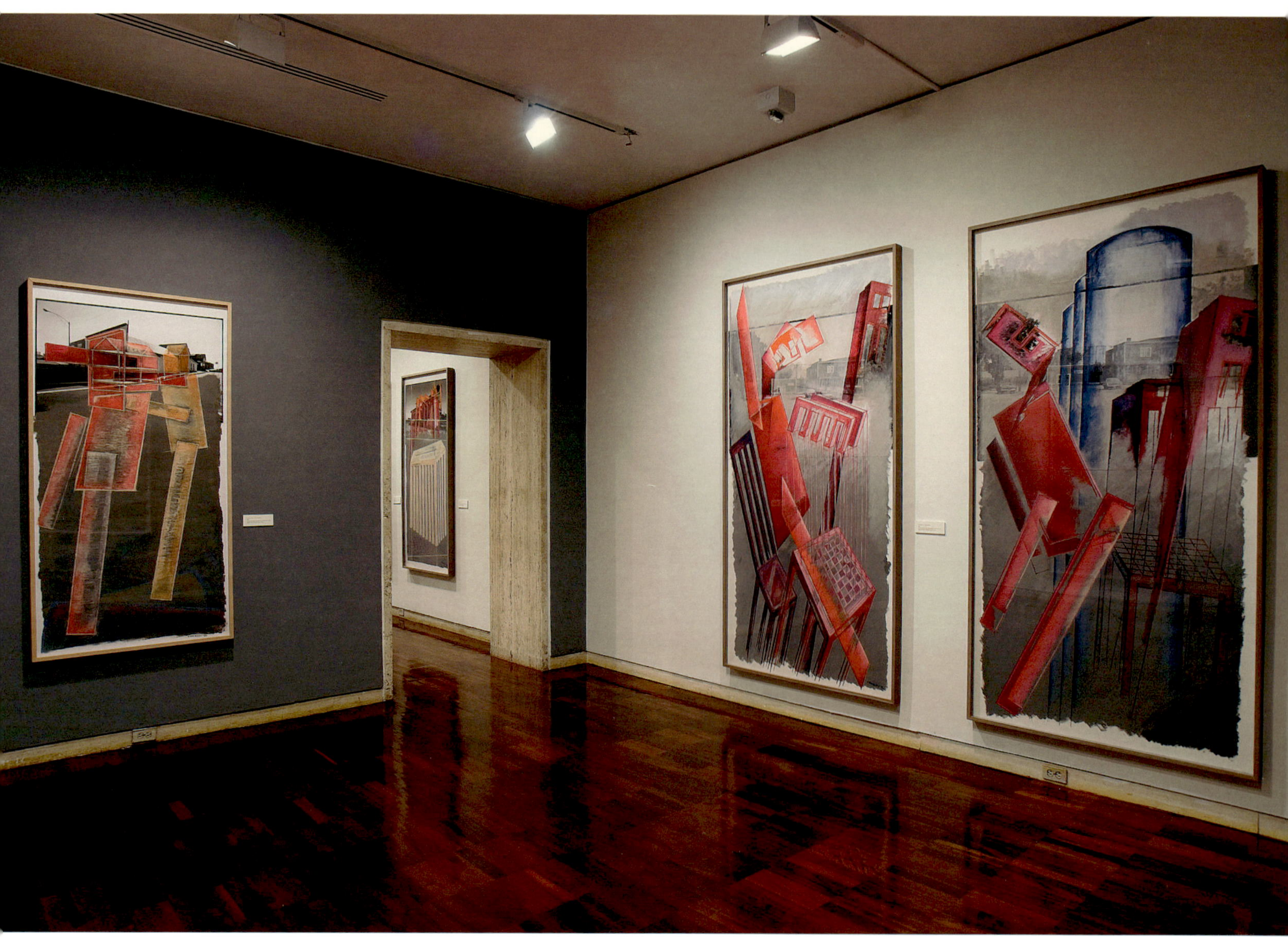

Between Observation and Intervention: The Painted Photographs of Melvin Charney, Americas Society, 2008. Installation view including the following artwork (left to right): *In Flight... de Stijl as a Prairie Dog*, 1990; *Parable No. 3... La Prairie*, 1990; *Parable No. 5... Trois-Rivières*, 1900; and *Parable No. 6... Trois-Rivières*, 1990. Photo: Arturo Sanchez.

Reading Melvin Charney

GWENDOLYN OWENS

The photographer as an artist is an observer, a witness, obliged to remain outside the melee. The orientation changes in the creation of an art conceived for public spaces—artworks inserted into the living fabric of the city. This tension between observation and intervention highlights and defines my work.[1]

Melvin Charney

Over the course of his career, Melvin Charney has created a body of work on the frontier of art and architecture, making photographs, sculptures, installations, constructions, and gardens that take the city itself as a measure of our urban condition. He is an artist and an architect, a teacher and a theorist, an observer and an intervener. He sees relationships in what appear at first to be unrelated structures, such as ancient Greek temples and run-of-the-mill, vernacular houses, and in his work he strikes parallels between such things as oversized buildings and oversized corporate egos. He is an investigator of metaphors in everyday language as well as in the language of art. His built work is informed by his knowledge of site and history, and also by his role as a planner (and quite possibly a proselytizer) who calls our attention to "one fit sizes all" buildings. All his roles inform each other continuously: what he observes with his artist's sensitive eye informs what he does as an architect, and conversely his direct experience with built work affects how he approaches painting, photography, and sculpture.

But it does not end there. As an essential part of his practice, Charney analyzes and critiques his own work, telling his audience what he hopes they will observe. In all his catalogues, including this one, he reveals his intentions through notes, interviews, or essays, often including his sources and inspirations and always assuming a high degree of sophistication on the part of his readers. (For example, not every reader would instantly be able to conjure an image of one of Kasimir Malevich *architectones* or an Edward Kienholz sculpture, both of which Charney has nevertheless made reference to in descriptions of his work.) In his writing he consistently rejects the divide between art as symbolic and architecture as concrete and functional, asserting instead that this border is permeable. "What has to be explained away is the notion that architecture has to do with functional objects," he once stated. "I deal only with built metaphors; and I do it systematically."[2]

Charney's painted photographs, a series that he began in 1990, are among his most visually accessible works. They are brightly colored with dynamic lines and shapes, and they make use of intriguingly oblique references drawn from everyday life. In each work he takes a page of text and an image from a newspaper or magazine, or selects one of his own photographs, and makes this borrowed image the starting point for a multilayered work of art. Imposed on the surface of these generally large-scale pictures are images both familiar (temples, houses, and skyscrapers) and strange (cartoon-like, anthropomorphic shapes that resemble buildings in motion; buildings with body parts; or buildings broken down into fragments). Often the buildings are stripped of their roofs and exteriors to make their infrastructures easily visible. The viewer can count the number of floors in a skyscraper, or see the depth of its foundations extending below the ground line. In other works one might find a geometric shape—which, as Charney explains in his studio notes, purposely echo elements in Suprematist or De Stijl art[3]—that seems to float on the surface of the picture plane. These overlaid images often reinforce the geometry of the image below it in the photograph.

As works of art, the painted photographs operate on multiple levels: one can read the layers independently, noting the underlying photographic image and the words on the page, and then examine separately colored shapes placed upon it. Or one can look at how the levels interact with each other—words relating to shapes and colors, and colors with other colors. It all combines in a kind of alchemy to produce deeper and more complex meanings: the walking figure in the underlying photograph somehow resembles a building; a series of roofs can in turn be read as roof tiles isolated from some gargantuan structure. The chessboard—which recalls well-known imagery used by the Dada artist Marcel Duchamp—can also be seen to represent the essence of the ideal urban grid of the American city, or the perpetual chess game played by politicians and planners as they determine the fate and the future of cities and their buildings.

Can erecting a tall building make a man more important? In these works, if one looks closely enough, one sees that buildings and people are both treated as living, breathing entities—sometimes even on the same scale. Small, roofless houses dwarfed by hovering skyscrapers look unhappy and forlorn. The tapering legs in the "running" buildings appear feminine. Are they female? Do buildings—constructed, like human bodies, from constituent parts—have a gender as well?

Melvin Charney came of age at the moment when North American cities were being blown apart, not by enemy bombs, but by their own leaders and politicians in the era of urban renewal in the 1960s. City centers were destroyed in the name of progress. Tall buildings were replaced by even taller ones. The shifting priorities and preoccupations of distracted city officials turned blocks of housing into urban voids as buildings were destroyed and replaced by nothing. Sameness begot more sameness as lazy architects and lazy clients accepted the repetition of the same building or building type over and over again. In Charney's art there is a fascination with change, not simply a critique. The works are fun and sometimes funny. Various "blobs" on the grid are overlaid atop advertisements for hermaphroditic "she-males" lifted from the back pages of seedy magazines. These sexually ambiguous hybrids are juxtaposed on the same page as images of equally ambiguous "blob" buildings, designed with no apparent relation to their site and seemingly useful to any client, anywhere.

Reading Pictures

Reading Charney's texts about these works, one learns the artist's view on his creative process and on the resulting artwork. About his *Parables* series, he writes:

> *The images in the photographs were loosened, detached and displaced. Places were reinvented. A narrative was engendered. Primary themes of twentieth century iconography emerged out of the images of ordinary buildings that I found in small towns and on the edge of the American prairie. The taut geometry and sliding planes of simple wood buildings stranded in the wide sweep of the land brought forth the planes of Suprematism and the sliding planes of De Stijl compositions.*[4]

Parable No. 3... La Prairie (plate No. 5, page 53), *Parable No. 5... Trois Rivières* (plate No. 7, page 54), and *Parable No. 6... Trois Rivières* (plate No. 8, page 55) each begin with a photograph of a house taken by the artist as the underlying layer in the composition. Does one immediately see what Charney describes above? Or must one first read his description to fully grasp his intentions? The floating elements that draw upon Suprematist imagery will be readily recognizable to those familiar with Kasimir Malevich's compositions, but what if one does not know the art of this Russian Suprematist artist? Can the viewer understand these compositions without the gloss of Charney's text? The building in *Parable No. 3... La Prairie* (1990), set high in the picture plane, is hard to read because it is largely covered by intersecting perpendicular planes in red and orange. Below is a severe geometric temple with square columns. The house is being obscured, it seems, by elements of architecture. Both *Trois Rivières* compositions feature a house, a car, and a one-story building beneath a wash of white color and set against various silhouettes: towers, walls, a chessboard. Can we take deeper meaning from this or just aesthetic pleasure in the formal elements of line, color, shape, and composition?

The point is that one can read Charney's compositions with or without the gloss from the artist. While knowing his intentions is helpful, it is not an absolute necessity. The names of these works provide a clue as to how we can read them. A parable is "an allegorical or metaphorical saying or narrative; an allegory, a fable, an apologue; a comparison, a similitude. Also: a proverb, a maxim; an enigmatic or mystical saying."[5] If we know the title we can access the idea that these are photographs of places that have been obscured by the elements of architecture—their own geometry plundered, taken apart, or hidden. By selecting vernacular architecture, Charney assigns these humble structures a particular significance, but the overlying architectural elements that obscure them simultaneously challenge this significance, making room for alternate interpretations.

As the series evolved and Charney began to use images from newspapers and magazines in his painted photographs, the possible readings of these works became even more complex. Here, not only images but words with fixed, assigned meanings contribute to the narrative and allow for deeper readings.

In *Clenched Fists, Greased Palms* (plate No. 14, page 60) of 1994, the underlying image is an illustrated newspaper story about post-war urban development in Vietnam. Close examination reveals a photograph of people on bicycles behind buildings that seem to descend from the sky above small houses that have no roofs, not unlike buildings that have been bombed. More traditional skyscrapers at the right of the picture seem to be leaning back to make way for the new buildings. We can see the newspaper headline at the top: "From Clenched Fists to Greased Palms." At the bottom, in the body of the story, we can read such disjointed phrases as "retain a firm hold on," "diplomats and scholars who frequently visit," "The Vietnamese have always accepted sacrifice, terrible sacrifice," and, finally, "Everywhere there are examples of corruption." This is a work of art about change from a world of war to a new world of western commerce, western buildings, and, accordingly, western-style corruption. The message is dire, and the descending skyscrapers drawn in red are definitely not benign. Yet, this is not a work that repels us. We are fascinated, not scared, drawn to the picture by the references it makes to elements of our own urban culture.

About the works from these series, Charney writes:

> *The dissemination of photographs by the media is now so widespread that important events in remote corners of the globe appear banal and meaningless when they reach us. Nevertheless, upon closer examination, images of the effects of an international economic blockade in the backstreets of a city in Vietnam or a town in Haiti reveal*

By selecting this photograph and superimposing images of buildings onto the surface, Charney is combating the way in which these images become banal and meaningless. He makes us look even more closely to read the words and see what is hidden beneath the colored shapes, challenging the viewer to think about what it means to take a country and impose upon it a city that does not stem from its own cultural traditions.

The paintings tell stories, and include words and pictures that allow the viewer to interpret them openly. *THE AMERICAN CITY: Ieho Ming & Friends, Manhattan 1989* (1999–2000) (plate No. 20, page 65) presents the image of a smiling man in a newspaper photograph; some will recognize this as I.M. Pei, celebrated architect of the Pyramid at the Musée du Louvre, Paris, and the East Wing of the National Gallery in Washington. The words in the newspaper story, visible at the left, indicate that the subject is urban development; more specifically, words such as "voracious appetite," "Manhattan," "46-story," "hotel," and "Park Avenue" tell us that this is about development in New York, and the picture suggests that I.M. Pei is some-how involved. The four towers in blue that seem to be landing on top of the lower buildings are shown without their exteriors; one sees the floors stacked upon the long, straight founda-tions that will be sunk into the ground to support them. And what about the blocky, squat buildings already there? The newer, taller buildings will no doubt replace them.

The *CITIES ON THE RUN* series again uses (or reuses) photographs that Charney had taken in earlier years. In reading these works such as *CITES ON THE RUN... on the edges of industrial belts* (2002–05) (plate No. 27, page 70), the buildings look like animated characters standing on their foundational piers, here bent at a point that corresponds roughly to a human knee, with horizontal banding representing the upper stories. They are on the move, slipping out of town on their leg-like pilings, making the decision to abandon a decaying city, acting on their own behalf to leave a place that no longer wants or needs them. In the background is an old city, perhaps Old Montréal, from a photograph taken years before by Charney. The static buildings in the photograph seem silent, abandoned, and unhappy that they, too, are not run-ning away. The work seems to pose a question: if buildings could "vote with their feet," would they choose to leave the dejected corners of the city?

Certain more recent works are tougher, dealing with issues of sexuality: "she-males" in *One Fit Sizes All/3: Blobs on the Grid* (2002) (plate No. 30, page 72) and racy bra advertisements in *One Fit Sizes All/1: Précis des Leçons d'Architecture, 1819, Combinaisons de Combles* (1999–2001) (plate No. 23, page 68) and *One Fit Sizes All/2: 20th Century New York Skyscrapers* (1999–2001) (plate No. 24, page 69). What is the relationship between the advertisements and the architec-ture? Here the readings are not so obvious. Twin breasts can be seen to correspond to the Twin Towers in *20th Century New York Skyscraper*; in *Précis des Leçons* a silhouette of a basic house with a pitched roof is repeated with a series of twenty increasingly larger and more elaborate houses, again layered over advertisements of intimate wear.

Today, it is difficult to separate an image of the World Trade Center towers from the tragic events of September 11, 2001, and the heroic place they now occupy in the minds of many. But, in the 1960s a neighborhood was destroyed to make way for the Twin Towers. The overly large towers that replaced the eighteenth- and nineteenth-century factories, houses, apartments, stores, and hotels had little relationship to their surroundings and did not do anything to enhance the lives of the people who lived and worked in the area; they symbolized for many the failure of modern architecture to address the human nature of cities and the need to keep to human scale in mind. In Charney's image, on the left, the towers loom in their entirety, dwarfing the surrounding buildings; on the right, one tower in superimposed atop other skyscrapers built in more diverse styles. Taken as emblems of a time before the events to which they are now inexorably linked, the towers warned of a less interesting future in architecture where too many buildings could not make up in height for what they lacked in planes, curves, or a harmonious relationship to their surroundings. If all architecture moves to *"One Fit Sizes All"* sameness, it results in a cityscape that is far less complex visually.

And what of the increasingly complex series of houses in *Précis des Leçons*? Here, in the same way that the bra advertisements show a variety of styles for the women who buy them, the range of house plans show a variety of options for people looking to buy a new home, suggesting that, on an individual level, we have choices for the same purpose. So while Charney uses one work in this series to show us that skyscrapers can have little relation to their site, he uses another to address those options that are all meant to meet the same universal need. The exterior of a house is simply a fancy cover for what is at its heart: just shelter.

When we look at them long enough, Charney's painted photographs thus awaken new associations—sameness and difference, relative size, and underlying structure—perhaps even inspiring a new reading of the actual cityscape outside the gallery. *THE AMERICAN CITY: via Saigon* (1999–2001) (plate No. 21, page 66) depicts three ultra-modern, curved skyscrapers: architecture of the post-rectilinear Twin Towers era. Charney shows us that the sinuous curves are just a thin veneer covering the traditional engineering of a standard tall building, with its straight, rectilinear structure of perpendicular uprights and flat rectangular floors. *One Fit Sizes All/4: From J.L. Durand to Manhattan Skyscraper Culture* (2002) (plate No. 22, page 67) shows an evolution of increasingly modernist building shapes that emerge from the basic upright slab, employing a conceit similar to that used by Pierre Matisse in his increasingly abstract studies of a woman's back (*Back I–IV*, Museum of Modern Art, New York). Just as Matisse's sculpted woman retained her essential form as she moved ever closer to full abstraction, so do Charney's buildings retain their essential infrastructure as they take on an increasingly modernist cloaking.

The Sources

All these associations that Melvin Charney puts into his art, both consciously and subconsciously, stem from a wealth of knowledge about art and architecture. A keen observer from the beginning, Charney began seriously and systematically to photograph Montréal even before he started art school. Many of the photographs were of Old Montréal, the oldest part of the city and the area that had long been its industrial and commercial heart. By the 1950s the area was nearly abandoned, as local commerce and industry had moved away from the port area in Montréal. Charney presents the streets dispassionately in cold, shadowless light as if the area was from another time, a ghost town. But there was a positive side to the presentation. Without people as a distraction, the viewer's eye can focus on details on the surfaces of the buildings or in the pavement of the street itself; we see details that we might otherwise miss.

Along with his interest in photography, Melvin Charney studied at the art school of the Montréal Museum of Fine Arts with Arthur Lismer, famous as one of the members of what is known as the Group of Seven, a collective of landscape painters who exhibited together and

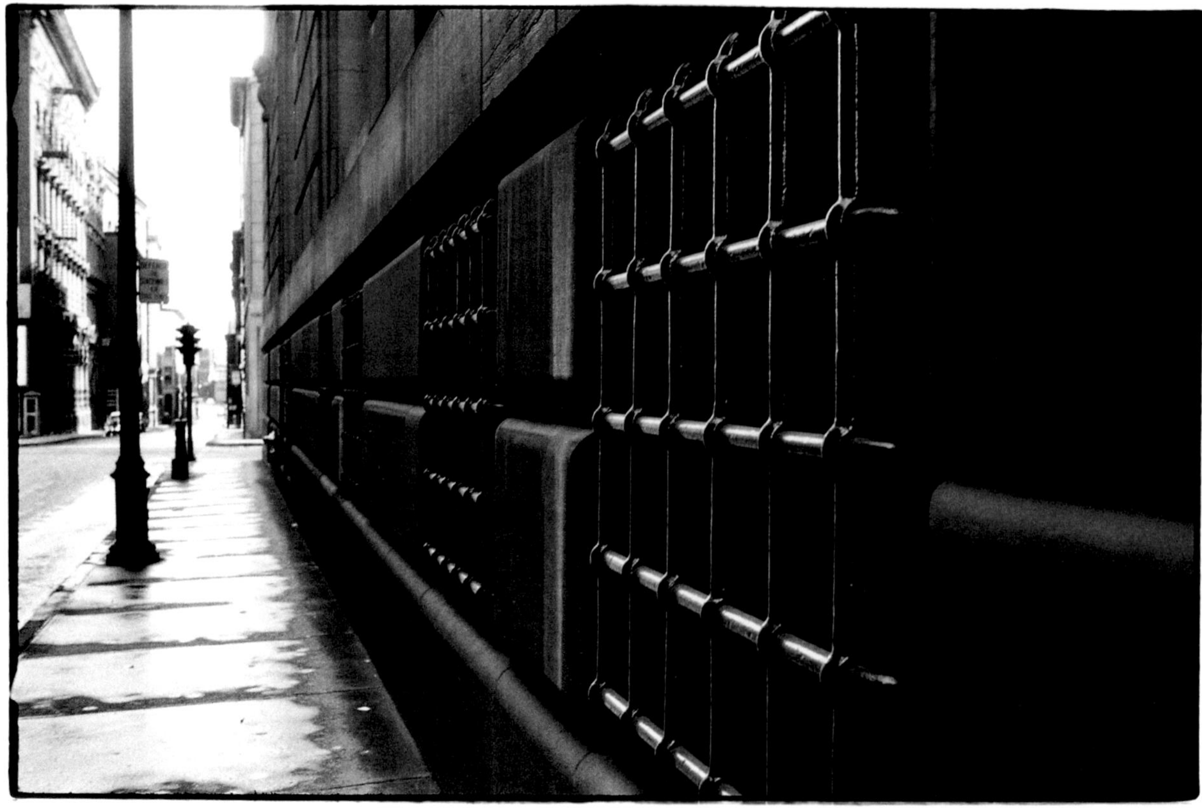

Rue St-Pierre, Vieux-Montréal, 1957. Gelatin silver print on fiber paper, 22.8 x 34.3 cm (9 x 13½ in.). Collection: Canadian Centre for Architecture, Montréal.

established a specifically Canadian style of painting the wilderness. However, having never met any working artists, he found that architecture seemed to combine his interests and abilities, and that he could earn a living by it. He enrolled in the architecture program at McGill University, graduating in 1958, and followed that with a Masters degree in Architecture at Yale University. Louis I. Kahn, the architect who was celebrated for his masterly use of light and his attention to materials in buildings such as the Richards Medical Research Laboratories in Philadelphia, the Salk Laboratories in California, the Kimbell Art Gallery in Texas, and the National Assembly Building in Dhaka, Bangladesh, was among his teachers; renowned architects Philip Johnson and Paul Rudolph (who was Dean) were also on the faculty. And unlike at McGill, where architecture was (and is) part of the Faculty of Engineering, at Yale it was (and is) part of the School of Art, which meant that Charney was exposed to artists as well as architects, including abstract expressionist Willem de Kooning and master photographer Walker Evans.[7]

As a Yale graduate with a degree in Architecture, Charney possessed the perfect pedigree to begin a great architectural career with a solid grounding in theory, practice, and engineering. He worked in the offices of prominent architects: Walter Gropius and the TAC (Cambridge), John M. Johnansen in New York (1959–60), and Guillaume Gillet in Paris (1960–61).[8] During this time, Charney also traveled throughout Europe and the Middle East, photographing what he saw and assembling a vast archive of images, which he used to make a living by selling them to magazines. He would also later use these photographs in his artwork, printing them as straight images, as constructed and combined photographs, or as composite layers in his painted photographs. His continuing photographic studies were important to the evolution of his thinking; Charney was interested not only in how the buildings looked, but also in their histories, their functions, and their relationship to other buildings and the surrounding landscape.

His first published article, "A Journal of Istanbul," which appeared in the *RAIC Journal* of June 1962, grew out of his travel observations and his photographs.[9] Sandwiched between an informational article about the New Canadian Chancery Building in Canberra, Australia, and a report on a seminar on hospital design and construction, Charney's article in the official (and no means avant-garde) publication of the Royal Architectural Institute of Canada seemed totally out of place, as if it had been parachuted in from another magazine. Based on his observations from his trip to Istanbul, the article described how people and buildings interacted and explained how difficult it was to see the details on the street because of the crowds—very different from his experience photographing deserted Old Montréal. Charney also wrote a careful description of the architecture of several mosques (not the famous Hagia Sophia, which is discussed only in relation to these lesser known mosques) and provided diagrams of their structures. His travel notebooks are filled with sketches and detailed descriptions about what he was seeing and doing, all of which grew into articles that he would later publish. At the time, there were very few Canadian journals in which to publish. Charney's work appeared alongside that of Louis Mumford and Alison and Peter Smithson in *Landscape* magazine, a quirky American publication under the direction of John B. Jackson. A shift in his interests can be found in his 1967 article "Predictions for Design."[10] It garnered the attention of the American Academy for the Advancement of Science, which invited Charney to be part of a committee that included art historian Henry Millon and famed statesman Daniel Patrick Moynihan.

When Charney returned to Montréal in 1962, the architectural profession offered enormous opportunities: the city was busy reinventing itself in a modern guise. Hundreds of new buildings were slated for construction, initially in response to the demand created by the 1967 World's Fair, and then due to overly optimistic projections regarding the future needs of what was estimated to be a metropolitan population of 4.8 million by 1981. (As this would be more than twice the city's population in 1961, it was indeed an audacious prediction.) But it did not stop there. By the year 2000 the population was expected to be 7 million. For architects and planners, the predictions offered an opportunity, while to municipal authorities they signaled an emergency. The predictions proved to be wildly inaccurate; by the year 2000 the population of the Montréal metropolitan area had grown to only 3.3 million.[11]

Rather than join the ranks of architects competing to build the new Montréal, Charney chose a more precarious career path that combined art-making with teaching and writing on architectural themes. As a professor at the Ecole d'Architecture of the University of Montréal, he organized and directed the school's Urban Architectue Unit, which played a crucial role in sensitizing the municipality—as well as generations of architects—to the significance of urban form. He wrote often and intelligently about architecture for a number of well-regarded, international publications.[12] With hindsight, we can see that his 1967 article "The Grain Elevators Revisited" in the British journal *Architectural Design* signaled most clearly the trajectory that Charney's career would follow over the course of the next forty years.

In revisiting the subject of grain elevators—enormous and impressive industrial structures dating from the late nineteenth and early twentieth centuries, and which such giants of modern European architecture as Walter Gropius and Le Corbusier considered to be modernist monuments—Charney opted to look inside them, explaining their engineering and including diagrams of how they functioned.[13] His desire here was not only to observe these mammoth structures, but also to disassemble and dissect them, just as he had done in his earlier article about mosques in Istanbul. He would go on to take the same approach in examining the inner workings of city planning and the evolution of the use of a site, ultimately applying this knowledge to drawings and constructions, something that came to be an increasingly important part of his artwork.

Charney's penchant for approaching questions about architecture and site from a more radical perspective led him to devise more unorthodox solutions, and to write more about theoretical ideas. His entry in the competition for the design of the Canadian Pavilion at *Expo 70* in Osaka, Japan, developed in collaboration with Harry Parnass and Janos Baracs, was to make a building in which "the equipment used to erect the building becomes part of the building."[14] When the Canadian Air Force proposed a competition for a new museum and memorial in Trenton, Ontario, Charney responded with a plan to diffuse the museum among discarded airplane hangars around the country so that it could be accessed by Canadians everywhere, not just those in Trenton.[15] Published in the American art magazine *Artforum* in May 1971, Charney's proposal comprised "a cross-country Memorial network by the installation of old aircraft or video equipment in centers of population, or the opening of old airports near several cities as instant Memorials where Air Force veterans could meet in the abandoned hangars."[16] Unlike his Istanbul article, which seemed so out of place in the *RAIC Journal*, Charney's article

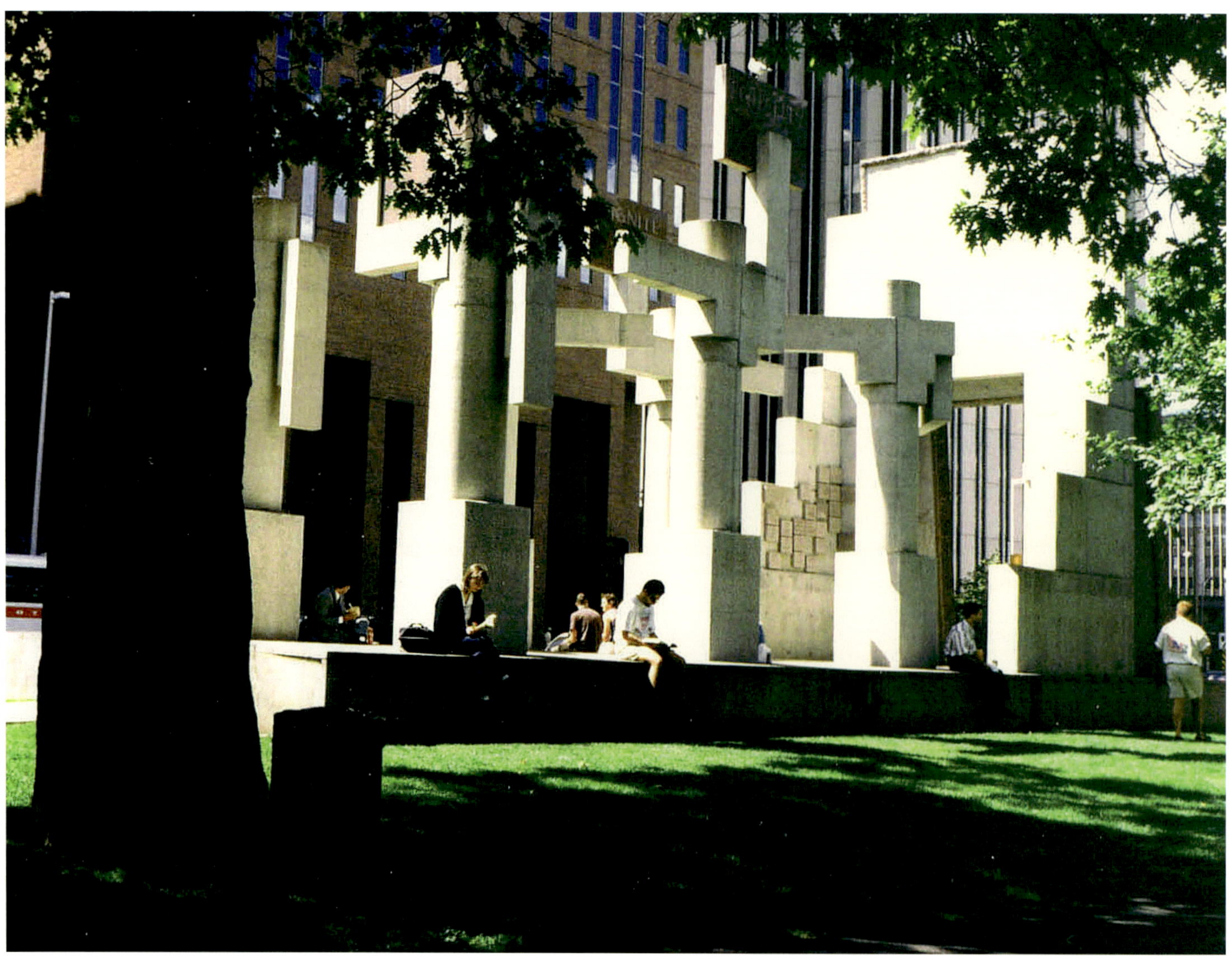

The Canadian Tribute to Human Rights, Ottawa, 1986–90. View looking west. Concrete, partially clad in granite, 10.25 x 5.25 x 33.5 m (33½ x 17 x 109 ft.).

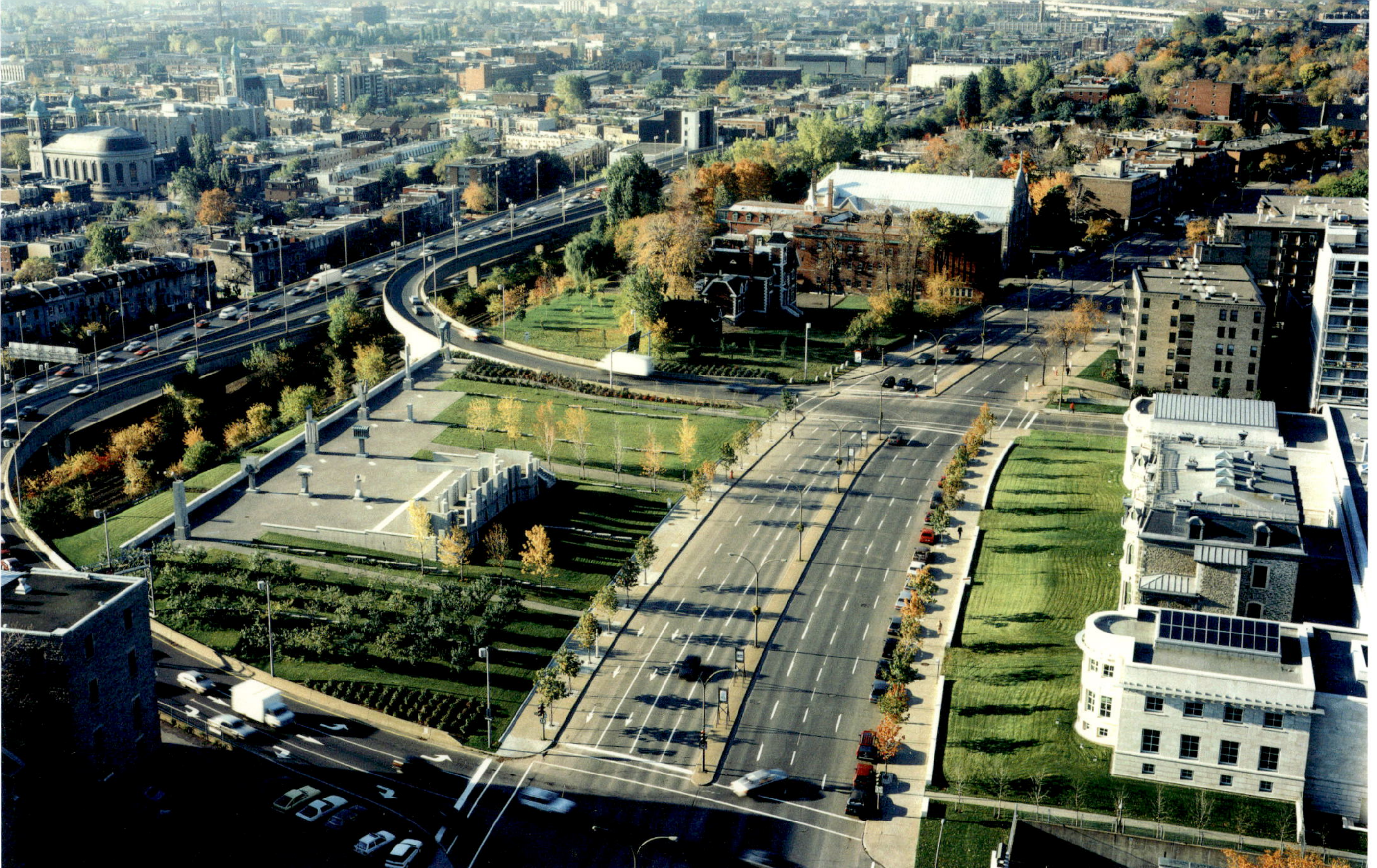

The Canadian Centre for Architecture Garden, Montréal, 1987–90. Aerial view from the northeast, the day after opening.
Photo: Mick Hales, 1990.

on his Air Force Memorial ideas was right at home in *Artforum*, alongside articles on Russian Constructivism, photographs by Diane Arbus, and an interview with Minimalist artist Robert Ryman.

Over the next decades Charney's concerns moved to the frontier of art and architecture, resulting in a rich body of work made for exhibitions, city interventions, and installations. He entered (and won) competitions for public art projects, among them the Garden of the Canadian Centre for Architecture, a sculptural installation in Place Émilie-Gamelin in Montréal, the Monument to Human Rights in Ottawa, and, more recently, the Esplanade Frontenac in Sherbrooke, Québec. In shifting venues for his ideas from conservative architectural journals to international, avant-garde art magazines, Charney carved out a particular niche for his practice. His understanding of the visual arts, as well as his works on paper and sculptures, were informed by his study of architecture and the city. Consistently thoughtful in his practice, he has come to be categorized with a small group of artist/architects (a term he usually rejects) whose work continually test the limits and boundaries between art and architecture, among them Cedric Price, Gordon Matta-Clark, and Hans Haacke.

Looking back, Charney's particular vocation now seems to have followed a logical trajectory. Threading the uncertain path between art and architecture was possible because of his training as both artist and architect. He had the skills and the experience to seek out projects for which he could not only make a work with visual impact, but also to which he could impart deeper meanings, using them as a vehicle for his boundless well of ideas about cities and modern life. Had he chosen to become an architect in the more traditional sense, he would simply not have had the opportunity to say all that he has been able to say with his alternative projects such as gardens or sculpture, where he has had the freedom to draw more directly upon history and art, nor would he have been able to suggest such radical ideas as his early proposals for the

Osaka Pavilion or the Aviation Museum and Memorial. Because his works of art, sculpture, gardens, and installations were not created in response to the practical needs of clients for shelter or for work, he has been freer to say what he wanted about architecture and to give those ideas concrete forms on walls, in sculpture, or in permanent installations.

The Built Metaphor

Perhaps the perfect metaphor for Melvin Charney's career is his project *Les Maisons de la rue Sherbrooke* (page 51), which was built for the temporary outdoor exhibition *CORRIDART*, a provincially funded art initiative built along the parade route for the opening of the 1976 summer Olympics Games in Montréal. Charney began by photographing a site at the corner of Sherbrooke Street (a street with the same significance as Fifth Avenue in New York or the Champs Elysée in Paris) and St. Urban Street, close to the center of the city and close, too, to what is traditionally viewed as the divide between historically French Montréal to the east and English Montréal to the west. In his documentary photograph of the site, Charney dispassionately recorded the nineteenth-century greystone buildings on the left and the vacant lot on the opposing corner. He then altered this image, flipping the negative and "repairing" the damage so that the three-story buildings were seen in reverse on the formerly empty corner, creating a symmetrical streetscape with buildings that mirrored each other. Printed in black and white so that the textures of the buildings stood out, his altered photograph resembled those of Rome taken by Fratelli Alinari and other late nineteenth-century documentary photographers. The altered photograph made the streetscape whole again, an elegant vista that was compared to the Piazza del Popolo in Rome.[17]

For the *CORRIDART* installation, Charney used his altered photograph to construct a full-scale replica, like a stage set, of the facades on the left-hand side of the street. Basing the project on his artistic vision of a completed streetscape, he built this replica in the vacant lot on the opposite side of the street, making what he had done in his photograph visible to a broader public. Over a period of several days, the Québecois filmmaker Roger Cantin recorded the construction of this installation, which was made of plywood panels hung onto scaffolding; he fortunately kept his camera rolling during the rapid deconstruction of the project that was subsequently ordered by Montréal mayor Jean Drapeau, and turned his footage into a short film that documents the construction and the demolition.

What was so offensive about an installation that covered up an empty lot and attempted to make the streetscape "whole" again? After all, the wholesale destruction of one side had hurt the other, as the side left standing was rendered incomplete. Reconstructing the destroyed side would thus restore the balance of the street. The mayor of Montréal, however, viewed any attempt to "fix" the hole in the streetscape as a criticism, and had Charney's *Maisons*, as well as all the other installations that were part of *CORRIDART*, removed from Sherbrooke Street before the Olympic parade began.

Charney, however, viewed *Les Maisons de la rue Sherbrooke* purely from an architectural perspective, with the idea of creating what looked like a city square; he was not making a statement, derogatory or otherwise, about Montréal society or politics.[18] Moreover, in this project based on the notion of "doubling," and, in the process, repairing the city and transforming a damaged corner into an elegant gateway, *Les Maisons de la rue Sherbrooke* serves as an apt metaphor for what Melvin Charney has been trying to accomplish throughout his career. He continually looks at both sides—at art and at architecture—taking what seems pedestrian and anonymous and infusing it with dignity, like that of an ancient Roman square.

Does it matter to us as viewers if we are unable to recognize all his references, sometimes even after reading his notes? Although Charney's words may enrich our understanding of the pictures, his works have a life of their own. Even without reading the notes to discover what he intended to achieve, the viewer can still derive meaning from what he or she has seen. Charney's works are not simply texts or lessons; ultimately they are works of art with color, shape, and line that excite the eye. One has the choice to read a Melvin Charney piece on one's own and to draw one's own conclusions, or to use the texts he has provided to pinpoint his particular sources and appreciate his point of view. One can also read Charney's text and still choose to develop an alternate reading as well. In these works, bold and direct and yet simultaneously very subtle, there is much to find, much to see, and plenty to return to again and again.

1 M. Charney: "Works and Commentaries," in P. Landry *et al.: Melvin Charney* (Montréal: Musée d'art contemporain de Montréal, 2002), p.158.

2 M. Charney quoted in A. Freedman: "Building metaphors—literally. Melvin Charney takes an unusual approach to architecture," *The Globe and Mail*, December 13, 1980, p.E5.

3 M. Charney: "Les Paraboles," in J.-F. Chevrier, *et al. Melvin Charney: Parcours de la Réinvention* (Caen: Frac Basse-Normandie, 1998), p.74.

4 *Ibid.*

5 Oxford English Dictionary (http://dictionary.oed.com); accessed June 15, 2008.

6 Charney: *op. cit.* (note 1), p.156.

7 M. Charney, in an interview with J. Donaldson, June 1999 (www.mcgill.ca/architecture/aluminterviews/charney/); accessed June 22, 2008.

8 *Ibid.*

9 M. Charney: "A Journal of Istanbul," *RAIC Journal*, Vol.39, No.6 (June 1962), pp.60–64. For a discussion of all Charney's early writings, see R. Legault: "'Pour une definition de l'architecture…' Melvin Charney et la modernité architecturale dans les années 1960," in *Architecture et modernité: Histoire et enjeux actuels*, Trames No.15–revue de l'amengement (Montréal: Université de Montréal, nd.), p.52.

10 M. Charney: "Predictions for Design," *Landscape*, Vol.16 (Spring 1967), pp. 21–24.

11 A. Lortie: "Montréal 1960: The Singularities of a Metropolitan Archetype," in A. Lortie, ed.: *The 60s: Montréal Thinks Big* (Montréal: Canadian Centre for Architecture and Douglas and McIntyre, 2004), p.77.

12 See, for example, M. Charney: "The Montréalness of Montréal," *Architectural Review*, Vol.168 (May 1980), pp.299–302.

13 M. Charney: "The grain elevators revisited," *Architectural Design*, Vol.37, No.7 (July 1965), pp.328–31.

14 M. Charney: "Notes for Environmental Design," *Perspecta*, Vol.12 (1969), p.29.

15 M. Charney: interview cited at note 7.

16 M. Charney: "On the Liberation of Architecture: Memo Series on an Air Force Memorial," *Artforum*, Vol.9, No.9 (May 1971), p.34.

17 J. Russell: "Where to see new artists," *The New York Times*, June 8, 1979, p.C20.

18 M. Charney: "Les maisons de la rue Sherbrooke," in A. Latour *et al.: Parables and other Allegories: The Work of Melvin Charney* (Montréal: Canadian Centre for Architecture, and Cambridge: MIT Press, 1991), p.69.

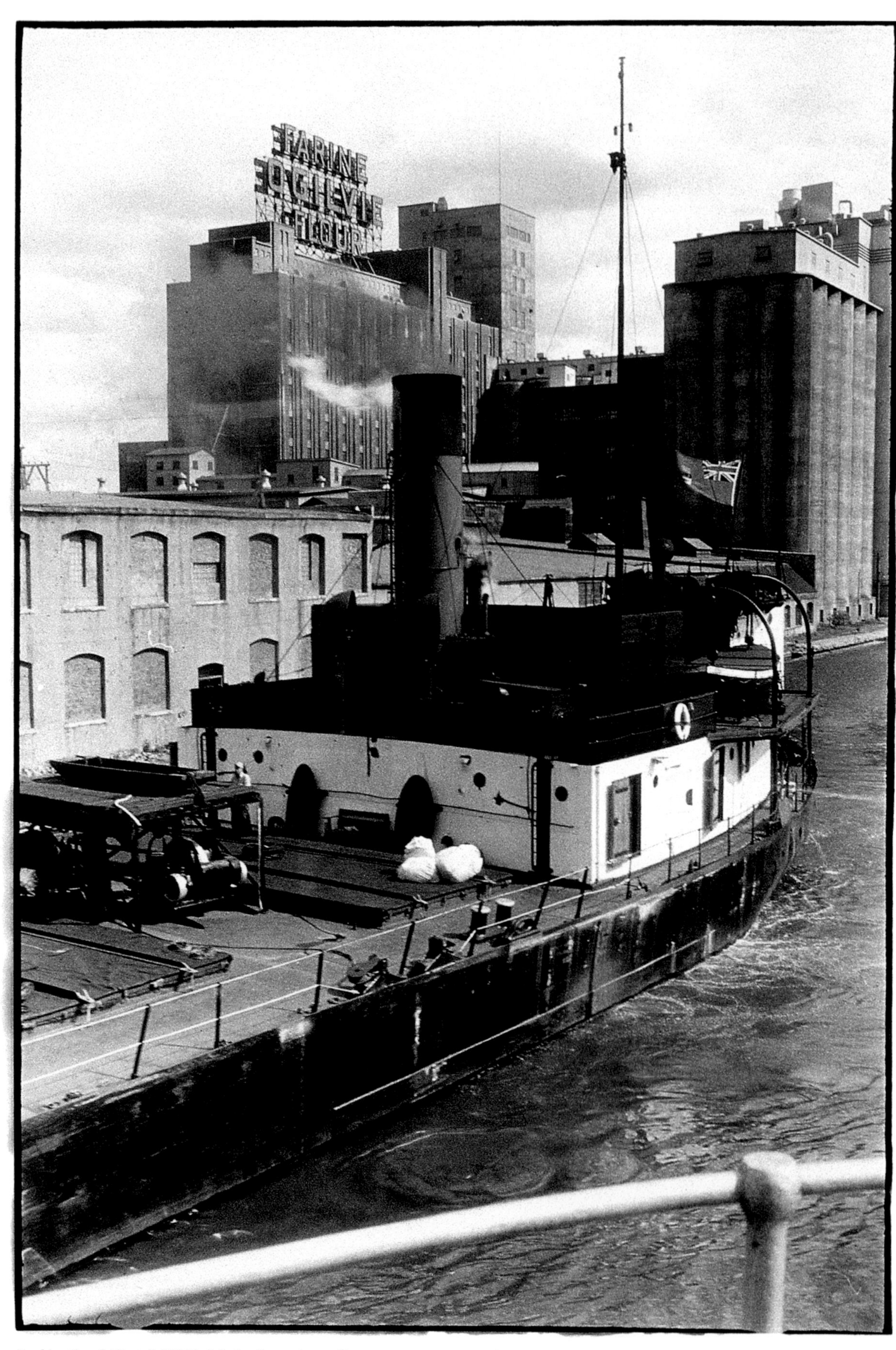

Lachine Canal, Montréal, 1956. Gelatin silver print on fiber paper, 27.8 x 35.3 cm (11 x 14 in.). Collection: Canadian Centre for Architecture, Montréal.

A City Differentiated   MONTRÉAL

YS I am so pleased that we decided to meet in Montréal. From what I see of the city, I feel that your work and much of its energy is grounded in the sense of place and people that mark this corner of North America.

MC Montréal, in January. A sense of impending crisis seems to infuse the city. Pedestrians carefully scrutinize everything as they slip-slide along icy sidewalks. [...] The three dominant cultural groups embodying the consciousness of Montréal—the Aboriginals, the French, and the English—have always been wary of one another, hardly tolerant of their compatriots' existence, yet peacefully disposed to one another in times of crises. And all of this is accentuated by a sense of displacement, an émigré's feelings of loss, as in most of the Americas, heightened here by a generalized sentiment of defeat dating from the end of the eighteenth century: the defeat of the French at the hands of the British; the subsequent defeat of the British by the Americans; the influx of Empire Loyalists who found the American Revolution too heady for their blue blood; the influx of Iroquois warriors and Hessian mercenaries who fought on the side of the British. [...] And even though these events may have long been forgotten, people in Montréal seem to live on a cantilever weighted by the past, and in one of several cultural spheres. The main issue is language. You are what you speak. A display of the letters on a sign—P, A, I, N—would send English-speaking Montréalers to a doctor, whereas their French-speaking counterparts would salivate at the very thought of a *baguette*. Most people in this city are aware, consciously or unconsciously, that the meaning of signs is directly related to shared language, ingrained habits, and cultural values. Signification is understood to be a human construct and subject to change, in part, by the will of the people.

YS Walking around different Montréal neighborhoods, I noticed that the housing is mostly attached row houses, in an arrangement resembling the long farms jutting out from the banks of the St. Lawrence River. I understand that Montréal was initially founded by settlers from France and re-founded, so to speak, in the latter part of the nineteenth century by French Canadians who migrated from rural farms to a burgeoning industrial city. This is a usual story for cities of the first industrial age in North America. In Montréal, however, streets appear to be different than streets in other American cities. What strikes me about your work is that it is underpinned by a concept of urban form. How did you arrive at this position?

MC I grew up in a dense urban neighborhood where lives and clotheslines abutted in close proximity. The notion of shared space seemed self-evident. The accessible city extended beyond my immediate neighborhood via public spaces, streets, and department stores—downtown mercantile cathedrals. [...] As a young person I was somehow convinced that an understanding of my immediate surroundings could serve me well and, contrary to a standard education in architecture, tried to ground my work in the reality of a given context. I still

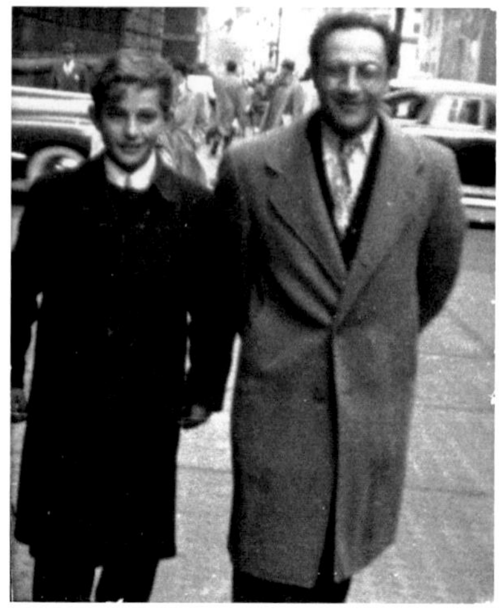

cannot deal with the idea that cities can be "created," *tabula rasa*, as detached entities, seemingly out of the air we breathe, and I am after a reasoned attitude founded on first-hand observation as a way of understanding a city.

My nascent years as an urban *flaneur* began at age seven, following Saturday art classes at the Montréal Museum of Fine Arts. I adored wandering the streets of 1950s Montréal as if I were on some mission of discovery. Later, I would associate the character of city streets with museums. [...] New York City was another one of my haunts. Most of my family on both my mother's and father's sides had arrived in New York City by the late 1920s, and we would visit often. I learned to use the subway and began to explore Manhattan and its museums. [...]

In my early teens I began to photograph Montréal in a somewhat more systematic way, reversing figure and ground. Streets, the spaces between buildings, steam shovels, and railway engines drew my attention, as did the processes and conventions of photography. What I had stumbled upon at that time were fragments of new urban formations emerging in the interstices of an evolving city—the transformation of the urban structure of a metropolis into a regional sprawl.

The underlying structure of Montréal can be readily extrapolated from a plan of the initial French settlement. It consisted then, and still does now, of generative and reproducible basic elements of classical cities found throughout history. Key elements are a specific house type with party walls, city blocks, streets, and squares as defined entities, all set within an undifferentiated orthogonal grid. In Montréal, beginning in the latter half of the nineteenth century, the advent of industrialization and the influx of immigrants, particularly from rural Québec, engendered a significant morphing of the basic urban house type. The traditional, iconic *"maison québécoise"* was radically transformed into an innovative response to the new conditions of urban life: a homegrown, three-story tenement, the "triplex," became the standard in industrialized Montréal. Unlike elsewhere in North America where lightweight stick building was introduced, the new system reverted to a heavyweight archaic encasement of three-inch-thick planks, *madriers,* in use early in the history of French settlement in North America. Nonetheless, with the advent of industrialization the traditional wall was transformed: lumps of stone were abandoned for a layered epidermis. The archaic sloped roof, with its death-dealing winter avalanches triggered by a knock on the front door, had its slopes reversed, its planes tilted to a central drain in a scheme that used layers of snow and air as insulation, yet in section resembled a Roman *impluvium*. Industrialization in French Canada invoked a sense of history, and people, in order to proceed, reverted to the same archaic techniques where they had left off in an evolutionary process prior to the British conquest.

The evolution of the working-class neighborhoods of Montréal resulted in a unique "rustbelt" of North America. What emerged was a primitive but highly adaptable shell of an urban system loaded with information that subsumed a potentially collective structure. With use, and from construction to construction, the structural shell underwent further differentiation. For example, a zone of elements emerged between the housing and the street—an articulated *parvis—* making visible a transition from the inside of a house to the outside sidewalk. What emerged was a dense zone of staircases directly connecting the front door of each dwelling to the street, as well as balconies, stoops, and entrances extending each flat outward into an intermediate

The artist, age twelve, and his father on the street near the Museum of Modern Art, New York. (Street photographer).

area, giving body to an evolving dialectic between the individual dwelling unit (the family) and collective, hierarchic forces within society (the street, the block, the neighborhood, the *paroisse*, etc.). A body of radically new urban formations assumed the guise of a familiar city.

YS What you describe as occurring between buildings informs the physical and social character of Montréal. And while people are housed vertically, each dwelling asserts some autonomy by maintaining an entryway, a direct link to the street. The disposition of these residential areas along factories and industrial spaces appears in a number of your painted photographs. Could you explain your attraction to these places?

MC My family lived in one of "these places." We adopted the habits of *quartier*-dwelling Montréalers and moved every three years or so from one flat to another in the same neighborhood. By the age of twelve, I could say that I grew up on the top floor of four different triplexes. Our sojourn in the second triplex, located on boulevard St-Laurent, three doors south of boulevard St-Joseph, is most vivid. On the ground floor there was a shop that produced and sold religious statuettes. Angels with gilded wings, miscellaneous saints—they seemed to specialize in a mini St. Joseph—the Virgin Mary, and, of course, several versions of the Crucifix. One summer, after haunting their open door, I was invited in to assist with the removal of the plaster casts from the molds: what auspicious beginnings for a contemporary artist!

I was, and still am, instinctively drawn to older, seedier parts of cities where layers of social pretension have long slipped away. The streets and buildings of the historic core of the city, known as "Old Montréal," and large-scale industrial structures dating from the initial period of industrialization, interested me, as did experimentation with borrowed cameras. And of all the industrial structures I saw, I found the grain elevators that lined the Port of Montréal to be the most impressive. I began photographing grain elevators in the mid-1950s. Much to the distress of my father, I would board European grain ships as they passed through the locks of the Lachine Canal on their way up the St. Lawrence River to Chicago or to one of the Great Lake ports, and I would hang out for several hours on the top deck or in the pilot's cabin. From the deck the grain elevators looked like towering clusters of geometric shapes pulled together by lengthy strips of conveyors standing on spindly legs. The conveyors were extended via mobile towers rolling on rails—"marine legs"—from which an arm-like bucket lifted and conduits reached into the holds of ships to unload or load grain.

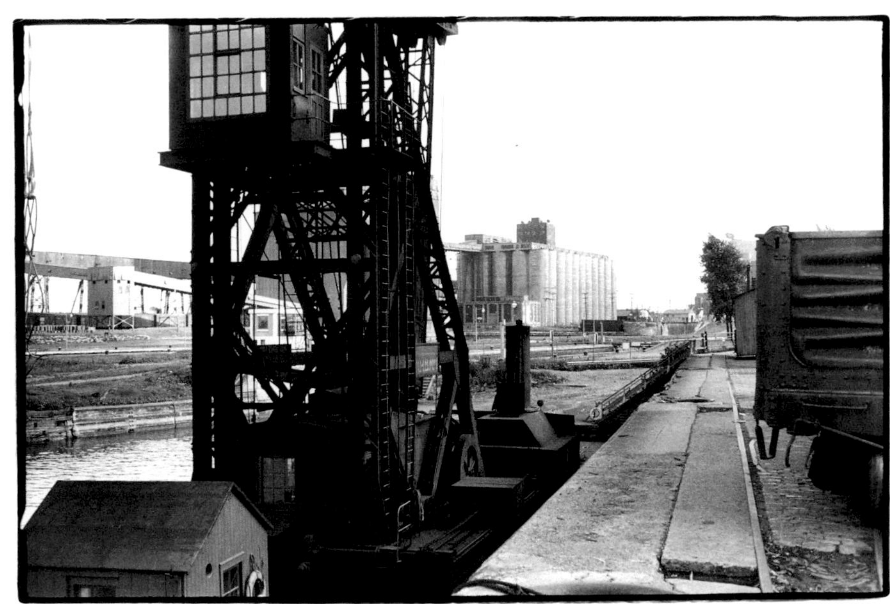

Entrée du Canal-de-Lachine, Port de Montréal, 1956. Gelatin silver print on fiber paper, 27.8 x 35.3 cm (11 x 14 in.). Collection of the artist.

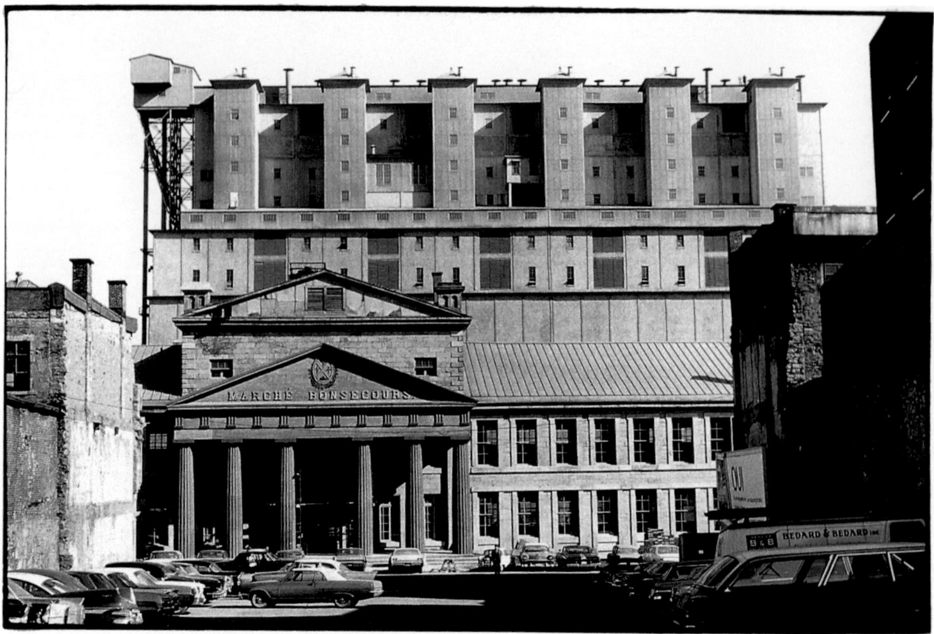

Grain elevators are located at transfer points in a worldwide network that collects and distributes wheat and other cereals. They vary in size from the wooden structures used by farming communities to the automated steel machines at transoceanic terminals. Within each elevator the grain is kept in a state of movement via conveyors and bucket lifts, as it is prone to explode if stored for too long a period. The movement systems within the grain machines still suggest a reinterpretation of streets as "conduits" for people. In Montréal the primacy of the street as a public passageway was heightened over time by differentiations such as a change of materials to line the street with a more "noble" revetment, i.e., stone, as opposed to inexpensive brick reserved for back and side walls of buildings. In other words the "facade" of a grain elevator—the primary surfaces of interface between grain (people) and the conduits (streets)—are inside the machine. The outside was no more and no less than an accumulation of the volumes of each of the constituent elements—a functionalist ideal of International Style modernism. [...]

The Collective Glue of A City   OUTSIDE–INSIDE

YS There is an aspect of your intellectual development that strikes me as particularly intriguing and relevant here as we delve into the notion of inside and outside. As you know, the "Islamic city" is characterized by a determination to maintain a division between public and private space. But what remains confusing about the "Islamic city" is that the street, the public space, feels private. It is often difficult to distinguish the path from the place: monumental portals are sometimes used to indicate entrances to major public buildings (mosques, schools, markets), but for the most part entrances are discrete and can be easily overlooked. [...] Are these "cities" as paradoxical and confusing as they appear?

MC Yes. The first essay I published, "A Journal of Istanbul: Notes on Islamic Architecture," appeared in 1962 in an otherwise staid professional journal. It included a drawing of the plan of the sixteenth-century Ali Pashiora bazaar in Edirne, Turkey, attributed to Sinan (an architect and engineer who, it is said, was responsible for every major building in the Ottoman Empire during a fifty year period in the sixteenth century). The bazaar consisted of a covered "street"

Grain Elevator No. 2, Port of Montréal (with Marché Bonsecours, St.Paul Street), 1969. Gelatin silver print on fibre paper. 27.8 x 35.3 cm (11 x 14 in.) Collection: Canadian Centre for Architecture, Montréal.

set in three contiguous city blocks. Once the subsidiary buildings attached to its outside walls were completed, as they are today, the Sinan building was no longer visible except for several entry portals. Composed of vaulted masonry corners situated between the walls of a square room and the circular dome that is inscribed within the walls of the room, the portals emulated parts of the building that could only occur on the inside. Within this composition, aedicule-like repetitions of the initial corners play with scale and depth, marching one's eye out to infinity, dematerializing the portal. In other words, Sinan created a significant urban structure that could not be seen. There is simply no "building" there. One can surmise from this example that some of the key formations of urban architecture are often constructs that cannot be seen. And if, as Le Corbusier maintains in *Vers une Architecture*, 1923, in the chapter entitled "Three Reminders to Architects"—illustrated, incidentally, by images of grain elevators—"Architecture is the masterly, correct and magnificent play of masses brought together in light," then how can the streets and squares, the structure of public spaces between buildings, qualify as "architecture"? Neither Sinan's bazaar nor city squares such as Place des Vosges, Paris, can qualify as having "mass" and therefore are not architecture. I would argue that the public spaces of a city constitute its primary architecture—its collective glue, so to speak—and that individual buildings are there to sustain the form of communal presences thus engendered.

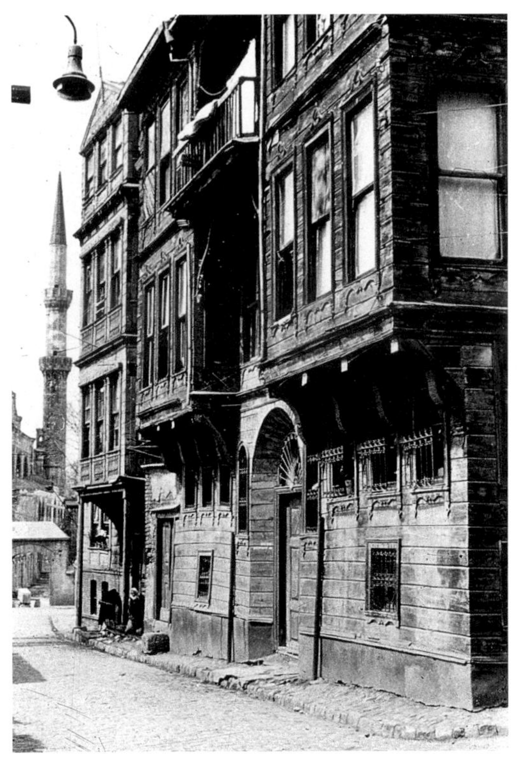

Istanbul, Near Hagia Sophia, Turkey, 1961. Gelatin silver print on fiber paper, 27.8 x 35.3 cm (11 x 14 in.). Collection: Canadian Centre for Architecture, Montréal.

Page from sketchbook: *Plan, Ali Pashiora Bazaar, Edirne, Turkey*, 1961. Ink on wove paper, 11 x 18 cm (4¼ x 7 in.).

YS Your readings of Le Corbusier's texts resound in the way you break apart buildings and float pieces of them across your photographs, tracing a trajectory. You perform a very explicitly critical, and often witty, analysis of modernism through the way you construct your painted photographs. How did you come to this way of interpreting and expressing your observations and comments?

MC Following graduate studies at Yale, long conversations with Louis Kahn and James Stirling, and a sojourn in New York City, I was convinced that the only way to move beyond the current discourse that was bogged down in a late-modernist cant was to step back and reconstruct a working history from "origins," and origins, as Kahn maintained, are to be found in the in-between periods when nothing seems to be happening.

In the autumn of 1961, with Paris as a base, I set out to circumnavigate the Mediterranean basin. After fourteen months I found myself in the town of Edirne, located a few kilometers inside the frontier of Turkey on the overland route from Thessalonica to Istanbul. Given the history of Edirne (it was the capital of Ottoman Turkey between 1365 and the capitulation of Constantinople in 1458), its strategic location, and its role as the setting of numerous battles, Edirne was still, in 1961, considered part of a "military zone." Turkish authorities were wary of foreigners with cameras and notebooks;

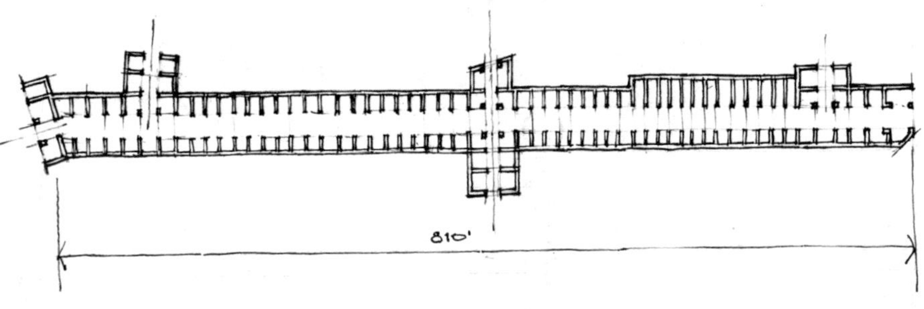

as the 1960 Hachette *Guide Bleu* put it, "travelers are warned that, apart from rapid visits to places of interest, or a stop at a cafe or restaurant, they may neither stop, take photographs, use field glasses nor leave the main road." The main road, its pavement hacked up by tank treads, traversed an austere and pockmarked no-man's-land leading to the massive fortifications of Stambul.

Dating from the Byzantine period, the fortifications drew a solid barrier across the land. Outside the walls, the scattered and dusty tombstones of Muslim cemeteries seemed suspended in time; inside a busy street life flourished under a sky pierced by minarets—including the impressive minarets of Sinan's sixteenth-century Süleymaniye Mosque. Conceived at the same time as St. Paul's Cathedral in London, the Süleymaniye Mosque resembles a cleaned-up emulation of the nearby Hagia Sophia. If one were to remove the minarets that the Ottomans tacked onto the already thousand-year-old building of Hagia Sophia—the Church of Holy Wisdom in the capital of Orthodox Christianity—what would remain is an ungainly and buttressed accretion of lumps of masonry, the order of which emanates from somewhere inside the heap. The Neolithic origins of Hagia Sophia are evident. An egg-like domed interior that turns in onto itself, with screened and diffuse amniotic-like light entering from apertures overhead, resonate as a presence in one's psyche, as do other such uterine palaces as the Church of the Holy Sepulcher, Jerusalem. Inside the Church of the Holy Sepulcher, the figuration of space is defined by a religion that affronted death with a promise of resurrection—the "Mother Church"—and, insofar as built relationships still define comprehensible models of built form, the public, urban facade of Hagia Sophia is very much inside. [...]

YS I have dedicated a period of my life to the study of this architecture, and this is the most perceptive and moving articulation I've had the pleasure to muse over. The way you describe the building's innards being turned outwards is precisely how this odd blurring of what is inside and outside transpires. I think you've hit upon the core of an architectural theory. As with your painted photographs and also a number of your public monuments, you show how an architectural form can be reconfigured. When you intervened with *Les Maisons de la rue Sherbrooke* (1976), *A Chicago Construction* (1982), and *A Toronto Construction* (1982), you filled

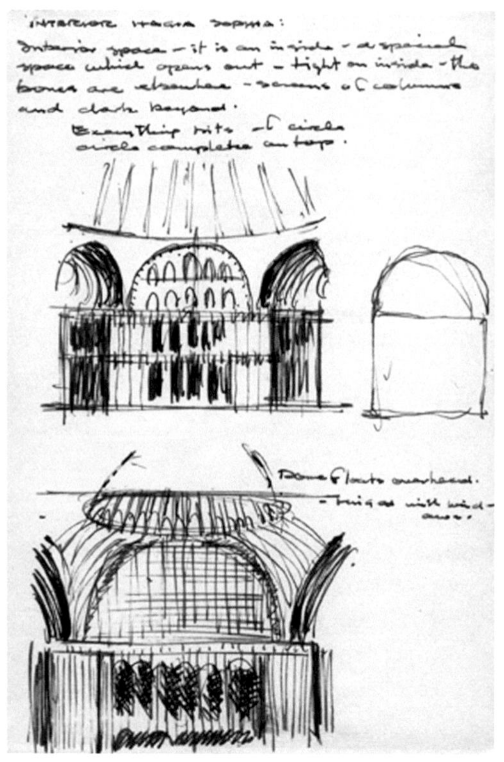

Page from sketchbook: *Interior space, Hagia Sophia, No. 1*, 1961. Ink on wove paper, 11 x 18 cm (4¼ x 7 in.).

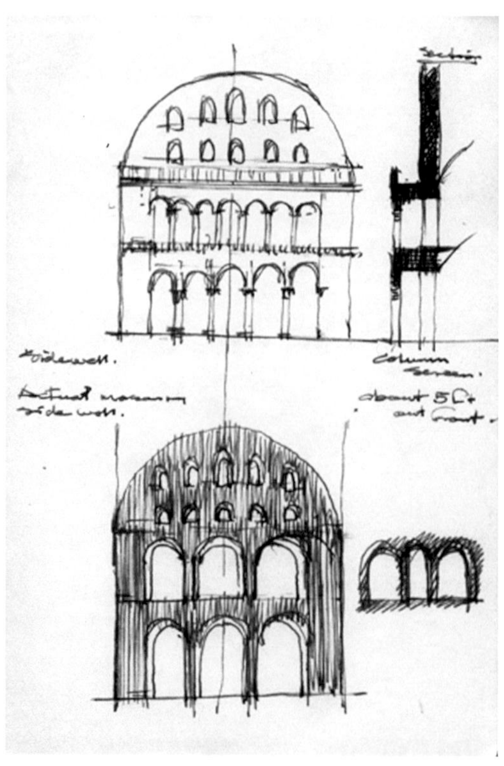

Page from sketchbook: *Interior, sidewalls, Hagia Sophia, No. 2*, 1961. Ink on wove paper, 11 x 18 cm (4¼ x 7 in.).

empty lots with constructions that mirrored something nearby or within eyeshot. What you highlight is one of the ways architectural memory can be activated and recollected.

MC Let us pick up on sites and buildings and on "memory [that] can be activated and recollected," as you suggest. Yes, I am invoking "memory," but memory to me is a given, a normative articulation of thought, if not the intrinsic formulation of thought itself. [...]

Religious sites and buildings in the Mediterranean basin seem to emerge out of re-formations of existing places and constructs that have acquired a rooted, autonomous, and sacred existence of their own. A gamut of religious tropes are found: from a 3500 BC burial device found in a museum in Jerusalem, in which a human corpse was placed for burial—and, hence, rebirth—curled into a fetal position within two halves of a clay egg, as in some Chthonic cargo cult; to domed enclosures of collective eggs denoting potential resurrections; to the Temple Mount, Jerusalem, where, standing alone on a raised platform slightly tilted toward the sun, the sharp light etches an overwhelming sense of responsibility for one's actions, as if in a Camus novel. [...]

From appropriation to adaptation, transformation to imitation, the specificity of religious tropes evolved from building to building. In Syracuse, Sicily, a Greek temple, the Temple of Poseidon, was transformed into a Christian cathedral by reversing the inside-outside relationship between the building and the faithful who frequented it. The Greek temple once stood as a sacred vessel focusing the surrounding land formations into a representation of a God, picking up threads of persistent Chthonic rituals while people remained outside its precinct, whereas in the church people congregated in an otherworldly interior to partake in the ritual of a resurrection—rebirth—of their savior. Attached to the front of the temple is a "building of entry," representing a passage through a mnemonic device—similar to the frontispiece introducing a volume on the lives of Christ and the saints—hagiographic instruction for an illiterate populace.

The Muslim appropriation of sacred buildings engendered other re-formations. In Cordoba, Spain, a church—originally derived from the columned temples of Egypt and Greece in which rows of columns describe an allegorical "sacred grove" or "Hall of Mysteries"—was converted into a mosque. These "Halls of Mystery" were eventually relegated to the somber, crypt-like halls that can be found in the lower levels of churches (as in San Miniato al Monte in Florence), as if they belonged to some buried past. Inside these "Halls," as in the church at Cordoba, a diffuse light bathed the rows of columns and drew the eye away along a multitude of darkened vanishing points; infinity was inside the church. With the transformation of the church into a mosque, a source of light was introduced at the apex of each row of columns, dissolving the interior. The building is at once both there and not there, an appropriation of an appropriation.

Inside the mosque of Hagia Sophia, again a re-appropriation of a borrowed building, an all-embracing light replaces the filtered, amniotic-like light in the suffocating belly of the Mother Church. Instead of floating in the vagaries of a church's domed and dripping belly—as in the Church of the Holy Sepulcher—visitors to the interior of the mosque experience an abstract otherworldliness defined by strong, direct light, and the space designed for worshippers is clearly delineated, contained between a flat plain of rugs and a low-hanging, horizontal filigree of wires, suspended lights, and calligraphic medallions. The materiality of mosques is rather tenuous, tentative, gestural, transitional, and certainly not urban in the classical sense of a city.

In Istanbul, 1911, Le Corbusier revealed in his sketchbooks an obsessive struggle to fit the exterior mass of Hagia Sophia into some kind of compositional framework. He drew it over and over again so that its masonry bulk would fit some canon of architecture. And so it was with the grain elevators. On the page facing his definition of architecture (noted above) is an illustration of *Grain Elevator No. 2* in the Port of Montréal, recently demolished. The illustration was based on a photograph of this elevator under construction, which was first published in 1908 in *Engineering News* (McGraw Hill, New York) and reprinted by Walter Gropius in the 1913 *Deutscher Werkbund* yearbook. Le Corbusier altered the photograph by drawing over the unfinished structure so that it would assume the hard-edged composition of a symmetrical building. Within a few years, the analogy of the grain elevator had been transformed into a building type that qualified as having the "look" of modern architecture.

Inside–Outside *STREETWORK*

YS Regarding this line between outside and inside, public and private, I was looking at a fascinating installation called *Streetwork* that you constructed in 1978 at the Art Gallery of Ontario, Toronto. You inserted a wall through the museum and continued it out into the street. The wall destabilized how we read inside and outside. You were challenging modern architecture's desire to efface the identity of an interior as being different from an exterior, the street—a question that repeatedly surfaces in your work. The AGO project in particular strikes a chord with me. You were doing something entirely different from what Gordon Matta-Clark was up to. And given that I work at Storefront, with its iconic facade designed by Steven Holl and Vito Acconci in 1994, and which attempts to tackle this same issue, I would love to better understand how you arrived at the concept.

MC An outside-inside conundrum is turning out to be a central theme of our conversation. This distinction should also elucidate issues prevalent in the photo-paintings, from an appreciation of the surface of an image—the outside—to the extraction of another image from the interior—the inside—of that image. [...] I usually proceed from project to project in a flow of ideas that percolate and evolve from one work to the next. Nevertheless, from time to time, and for various reasons, I may slip into a black hole that tends to dissipate my energy and absorb all thought. The AGO piece was snagged from the vortex of one such black hole that I, unwittingly, got caught up in. [...]

After working for several years on an ongoing project involving the front pages of newspapers—*UN DICTIONNAIRE...*(1970–2001)—I was commissioned by Montréal's 1976 Olympic Games Committee to put together a 1.5-km exhibition of art along one of the city's main thoroughfares leading to the Olympic Stadium. Five days after the opening of the exhibition, on the evening prior to the opening of the Olympic Games, the mayor of Montréal ordered municipal authorities to demolish the show. The drama made the front pages of major newspapers, nationally and internationally, including one photograph of the Olympic flag going up and another of the work coming down. To cover for his abuse of power, the mayor claimed that we had violated municipal regulations, even though his flunkies sat in on every one of our meetings and issued the necessary city permits. Later, in court, the Mayor would claim that he was obliged to protect the public from "blasphemy!"

The exhibition, *CORRIDART*, included the work of 150 artists, as well as a full-size construction-installation, *Les Maisons de la rue Sherbrooke*, which I conceived for a critical intersection. The destruction of *Les Maisons...* marked the culmination of a cycle in my work.

What began five years earlier, using images of events that appeared on the front pages of newspapers, seemed to come to an untimely conclusion with one of my artworks on the front pages of newspapers. As the victim of the political connivance of the mayor, I was systematically demonized as having provoked the incident, and it was difficult to work in the year following his aggression. Both artists and politicians juggle symbols; unfortunately, politicians tend to alter the artist's attitude of "now you don't see it and now you do" into "now you see it and now you don't." And then, in 1977, an invitation from the Art Gallery of Ontario, Toronto, to exhibit my work there was a veritable clarion call (plate Nos. 1 and 2, page 50). [...]

At the time of the AGO call, I was preoccupied with questions about "figuration," in particular with *Les Maisons de la rue Sherbrooke*. I was also musing about a dull, black-and-white photograph of a Kasimir Malevich painting, *Suprematisme Dynamiqe* (1916), which appeared in a newspaper alongside a notice that 1978 marked the centenary of his birth. I began the AGO work with an examination of the paradigmatic trope that generated the "figure" of the museum and of the exhibition space allocated for the show. I then proceeded to paint two similar intersecting planes over both the photograph of Malevich's painting and the AGO gallery plan. I then constructed a wall across an existing wall so as to pick up on the composition of the intersecting planes. It was an attempt to distinguish the underlying trope of the modernist abstraction of architecture, such as that of the AGO, which has long been cut off from its sources. The existing museum building did not so much house the work—contain it—as combine with it. The form

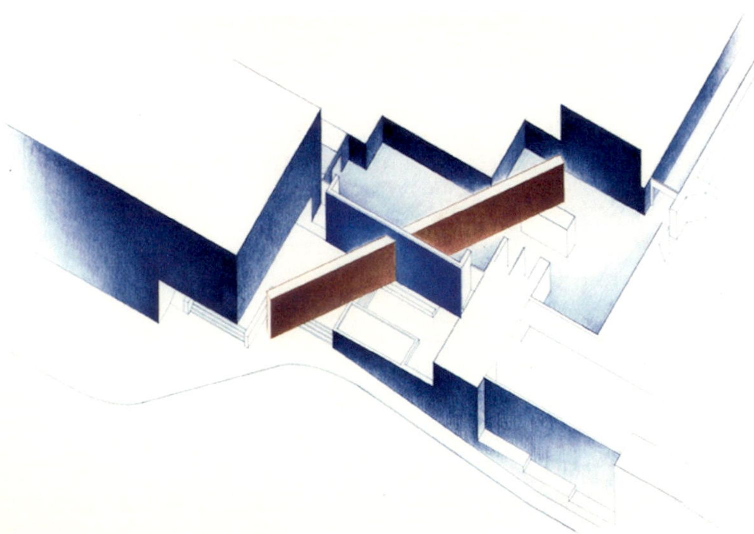

of the inserted wall changed according to its position and in relation to the existing building: outside, in the street, the wall was made to assume the form of an "arcade;" inside it became a series of partitions. In other words, a void on the outside (access) became a volume on the inside (closure). The construction opened the envelope of the building so that intersecting planes were extracted from its presence. Instead of moving out to infinity in an idealistic, modernist haze, as the legacy of De Stijl would have it, the intersecting planes drew the body of the building into a *Streetwork*.

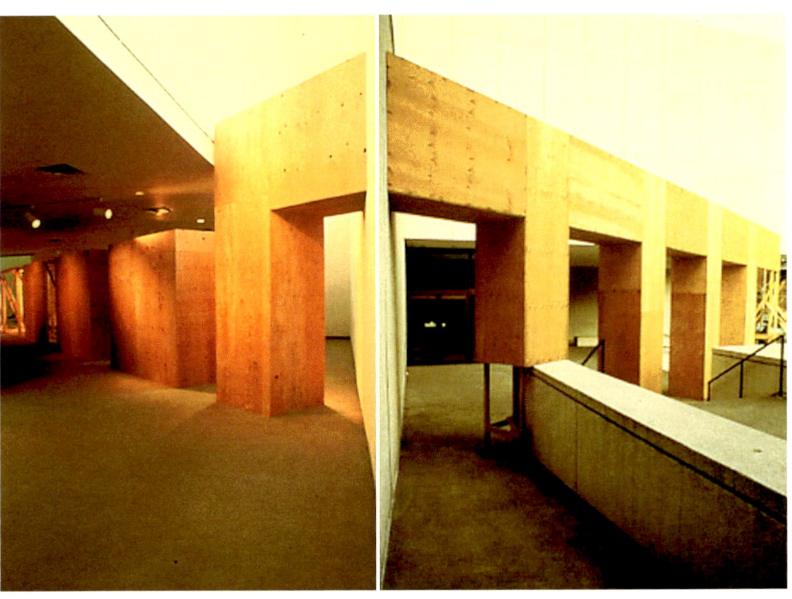

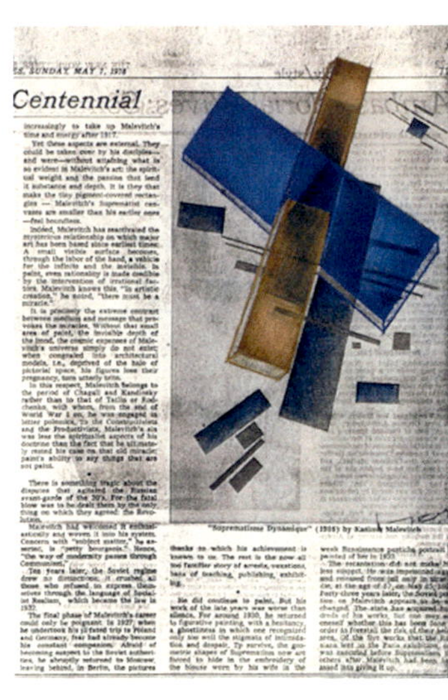

Another issue brought forth by *Streetwork* was the question of categorization: is it a work of art or architecture? The answer: both. Given that *Streetwork* was published simultaneously in art magazines (*Artforum*, New York) and in architecture journals (*AD*, London), it was considered to be art if seen in an art journal, vice versa in an architectural journal. For me, this overlap of disciplines has been going on since *MEMO SERIES* (1969–70). In order to get things done, one simply carries on with one's work regardless of institutional terms of reference that no longer relate to what is going on. […]

Art–Architecture   ON *MEMOS*

YS The way you live and the way you work embody, linguistically and practically, the notion of a "hybrid practice." You operate in two worlds, art and architecture, in that you make "art" and you work on public architectural projects. Somehow this has formed a meeting ground between the two disciplines […] and re-formed you into an artist, an intellectual, and an academic as well as an architect. I'm curious to know how these categories operate in the way you conceive projects and understand your practice.

MC It is difficult to categorize what I do. Even though my activities are not all that complex, the available words are too blunt, as if an ossification of nomenclature has taken place in the face of change. […]

In an essay on Oxford teachers of philosophy and language that appeared in the *New Yorker*, 1961, Ved Mehta comments on "questions like 'What is 'truth'?" Oxford philosophers are liable to say, following the late Wittgenstein, "Look at all the different ways the word 'true' is used in ordinary speech." So, let's look at the content of "ordinary speech" in commentaries on and reviews of my work, from curators, reviewers, and bureaucrats who feel they have to establish some kind of formal categorization for it. I am referred to as an artist, a photographer, and a sculptor, "*un peintre canadien*," who shows photo-based work, who works with oil pastel, and, of course, an architect and a landscape architect. In other words, the old framework of art production divided according to medium, with architecture as the "mother" of the arts, still holds sway. However, in the world I live in, the tendency is to focus on a sphere of endeavor where media is part of the content and "crossover" disciplines have become the norm.

In Paris in the early sixties, I worked four days a week for an architect, Guillaume Gillet, whose church of Notre Dame in Royan, France (completed in 1958), I noticed at an exhibition at the Museum of Modern Art in New York. The three remaining days of the week I would revert to my art. I found then, and still do now, that it is difficult to shift from one sphere to the other. I would begin by drawing anything in sight, a table, a chair, a water glass—*repose en paix* Morandi—but could not relate the social disposition of architecture to the general detachment of art. Each activity has its charm. As an architect I would compose my *oeuvre* and send out instructions to be executed—performed—by others, whereas in art, an object is said to pour out of the artist's fingers, a most gratifying experience. The institutional barriers that we thought would simply dissolve of their own accord in the 1970s are alive, well, and in place, and often enforced with a vengeance.

YS Architectural installation can be a way for artists to refer, superficially, to cities and buildings. In the same way, architects dabbling in art tend to superimpose onto architectural renderings

MEMO SERIES, Plate 02, Location in the Network, 1970. Montage of text, black-and-white photographs, Xerox, and lithography on wove paper, 54.5 x 35 cm (21½ x 13¾ in.). Collection: The National Gallery of Canada, Ottawa.
MEMO SERIES, Plate 20, Morphology of Air Force, 1970. Montage of text, black-and-white photograph, and lithography on wove paper, 54.5 x 35 cm (21½ x 13¾ in.). Collection: The National Gallery of Canada, Ottawa.

more engaging images than architecture can accommodate. Nevertheless, it is important that authentic practices that fall between disciplines be recognized. You bring to your art the expertise and experience of an architect. Could we talk through your work to discuss how you fused these two disciplines?

MC A discipline involves regulation, authority, and the application of a specific slice of knowledge, and if an innovative, "interdisciplinary" endeavor appears, it will emerge in the "doing" of a project. [...]

In 1970 I participated in a competition for the design of an Air Force Memorial and Museum to be located on a residual piece of land at an air force base some 100 kilometres east of Toronto. It seemed to me more reasonable to base a design "solution" on readily available sources derived from a world radically altered by technology—due in part to air flight—rather than contriving an appropriate look of a built container. A salient part of this process was the identification of "off-the-shelf" and in-use resources so that the Monument-Museum could become a network of parts, bringing a "building" to people across Canada. The resources were described in a series of memoranda, the *MEMO SERIES*. Each *MEMO* was conceived as a printed plate with texts, photographs, drawings, and instructions suitable to be shipped to the Department of Defence, the sponsors of the competition, for implementation.

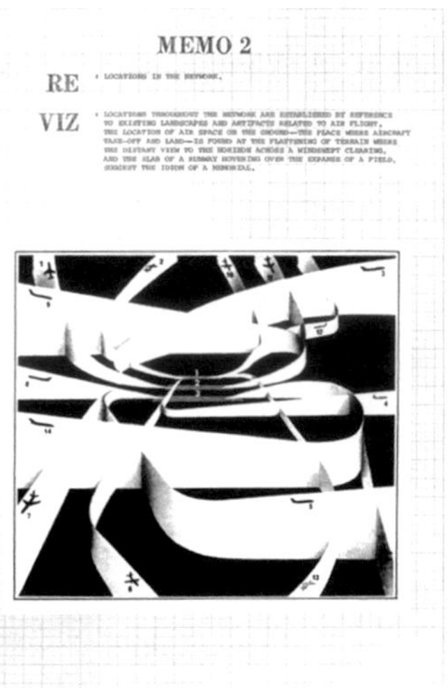

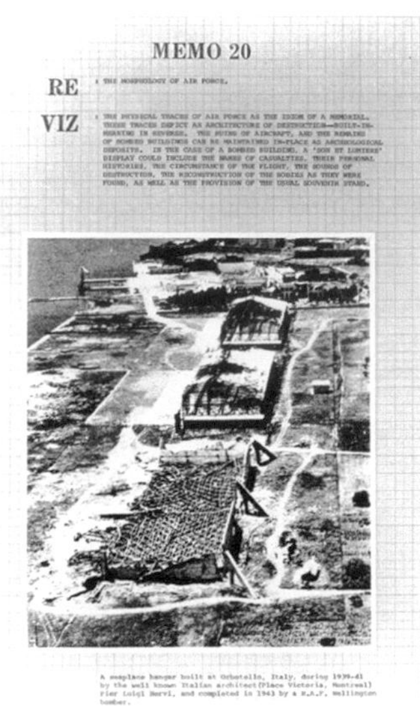

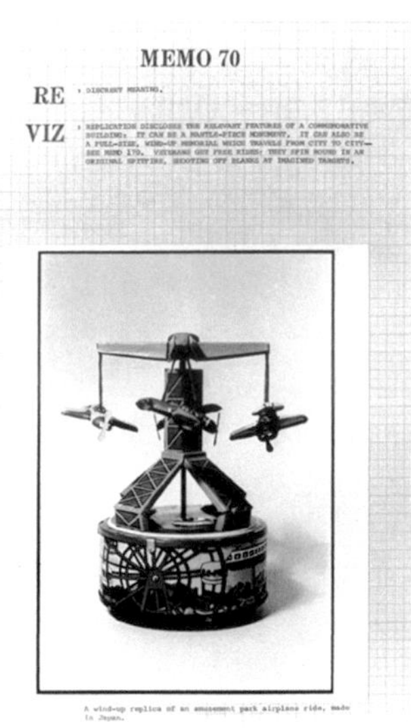

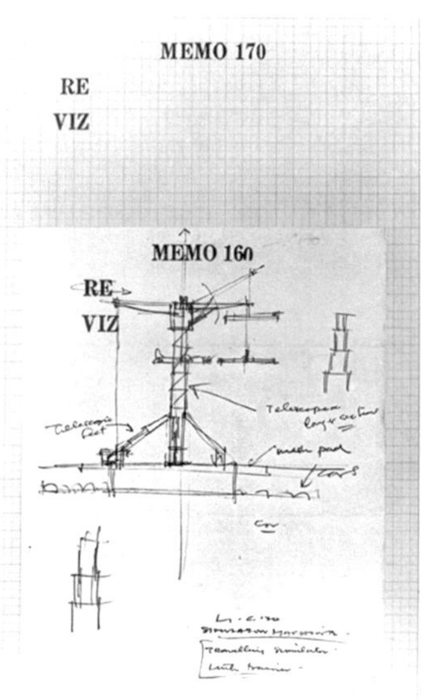

The series initiated an ongoing process of pushing at the edges of what was possible and seemed limited only by one's ability to discern new phenomena. The final count: seventy-four finished plates (thirty-two of which are now in the collection of the National Gallery of Canada). Key plates include a found map of scheduled Air Canada flights locating the Museum-Memorial as a network of available facilities that people can visit simultaneously across the country; abandoned hangars and their reuse as instant network outposts; and plots of land consecrated by the loss of people's lives that would become the locations of Memorial sites, such as the site of a Liberator bomber crashing north of Montréal in 1945. On another plate, an abandoned

MEMO SERIES, Plate 70, Discreet Meaning, 1970. Montage of text, black-and-white photograph, and lithography on wove paper, 54.5 x 35 cm. (21½ x 13¾ in.). Collection: The National Gallery of Canada, Ottawa.
MEMO SERIES, Plate 170, An Air Force Memorial Ride for County Fairs, 1970. Montage of text, drawing, and lithography on wove paper, 54.5 x 35 cm. (21½ x 13¾ in.). Collection: The National Gallery of Canada, Ottawa.

landing strip suggests the actual construction of a kilometer-long slab of concrete oriented toward the wind, with red lights set up at diminishing heights on top of surrounding buildings, like a Memorial where one could simulate flying by dashing down the runway with arms outspread. [...] Often, sources originated in media photos of news events, some of which I would overlay with paint and oil pastel. [...]

The *MEMO SERIES* began as part of my preoccupation with the idea of "tacit knowledge" (c.f. Michael Polanyi) embedded in the material formations of fabricated things—knowledge beyond the threshold of what we are capable of naming. By 1970 I began to collect and classify newspaper pages with photographs showing buildings and cities caught up in various events. Certain images would appear over and over again regardless of the events they depicted, suggesting some kind of order in the display of each day's news. From time to time a news image would provoke a sense of urgency to draw out from the image certain elements. [...]

The Painted Photographs   *UN DICTIONNAIRE...*

YS For over thirty years, 1969–2004, you have been compiling an archive of over 1,400 newspaper pages with images of events that catalogue the many ways in which our constructed world is represented in the media. How does the stream of images emitted by the media affect our understanding of the constructed environment?

MC Images emitted by the media tend to focus our attention on a particular building or city, and attribute a certain cachet of consequence to structures and places caught up in an instance of celebration or, more likely, disaster. The images depict a world in a state of distress, of flux. A crowded street protest, a house shoved off its foundations by water and wind, a building with its walls blown away all reveal inner supports. The layers of contrivance are stripped away. Relationships are uncovered, hidden connections exposed.

Recurring images suggest themes. The themes, in turn, propose a system of classification in which images can be grouped, roughly, in series according to what they disclose about the

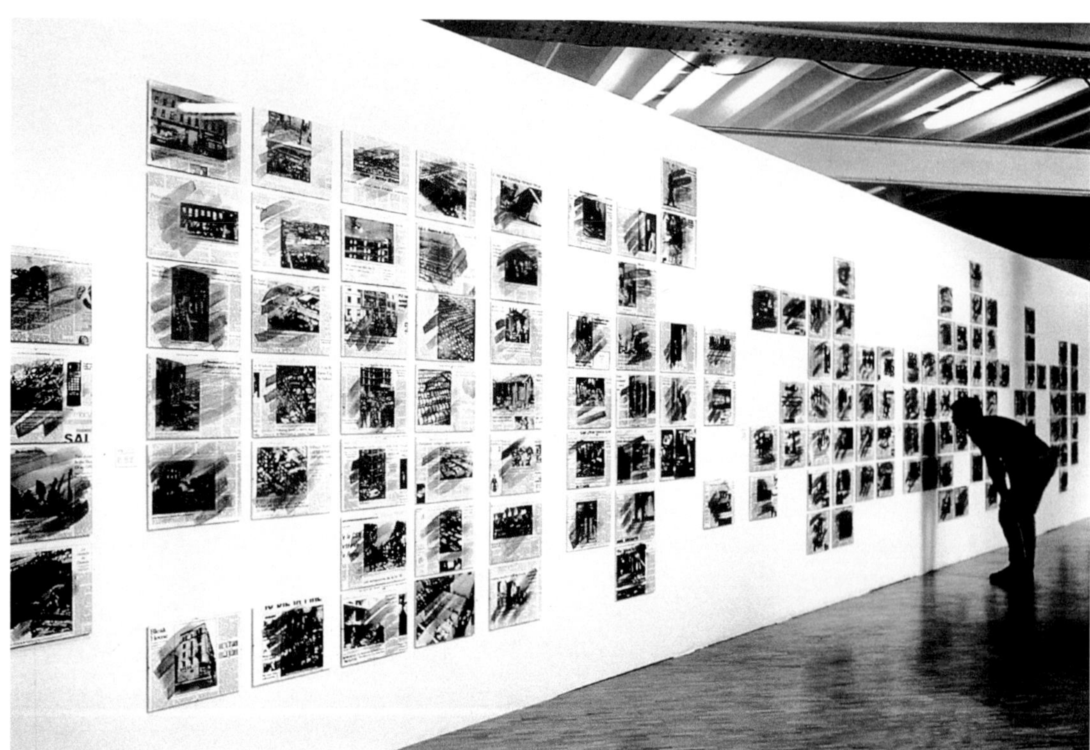

UN DICTIONNAIRE...
Illuminations, 1970–96.
Installation view, Fondation
pour l'Architecture,
Brussels. Photo: Philippe De
Gobert, courtesy Fondation
pour l'Architecture.

UN DICTIONNAIRE... is
composed of a selection of
newspaper pages, organized
as a series of plates. Each
plate is located in a vertical
column.

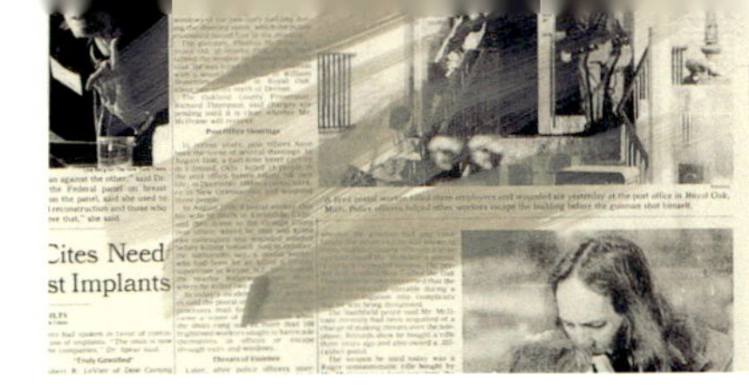
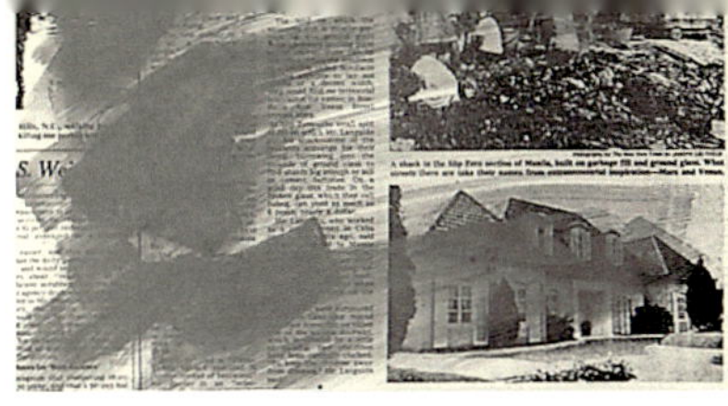
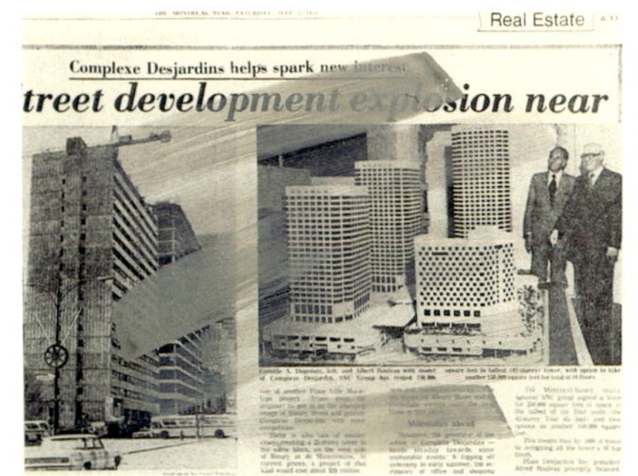
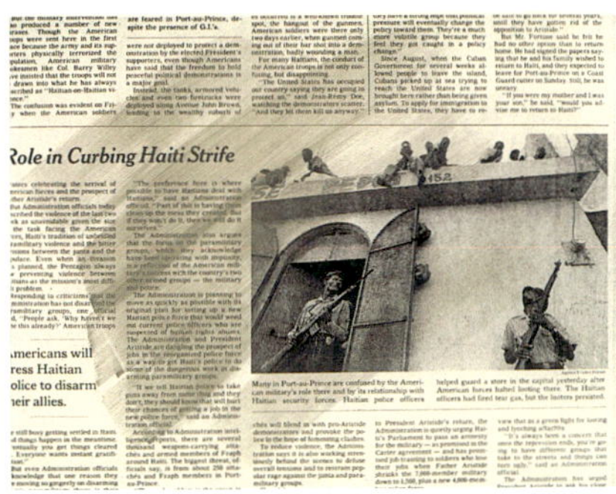
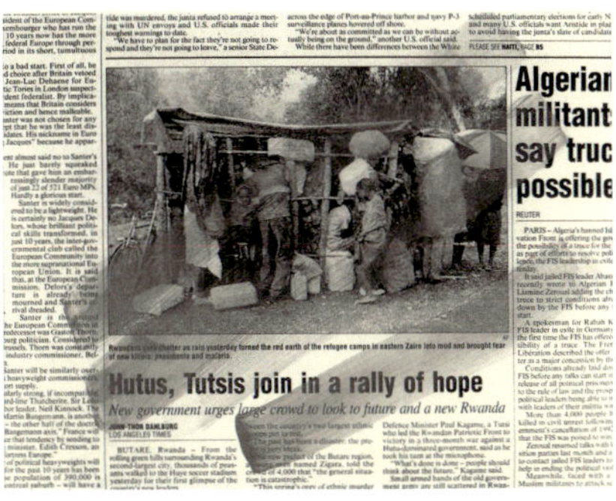
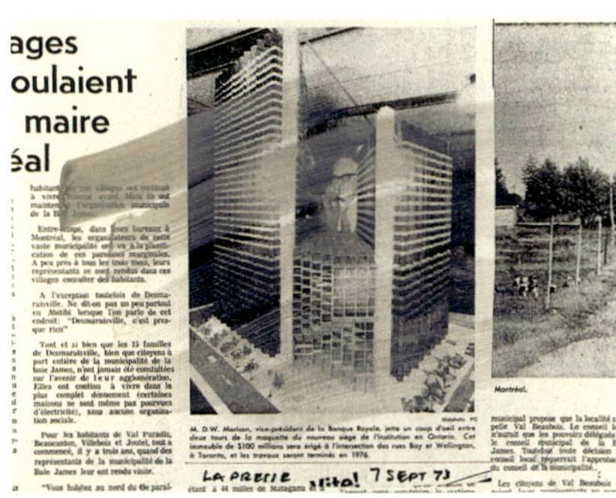
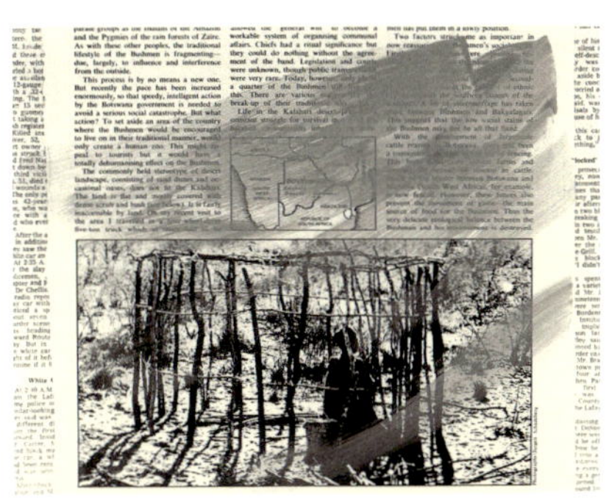
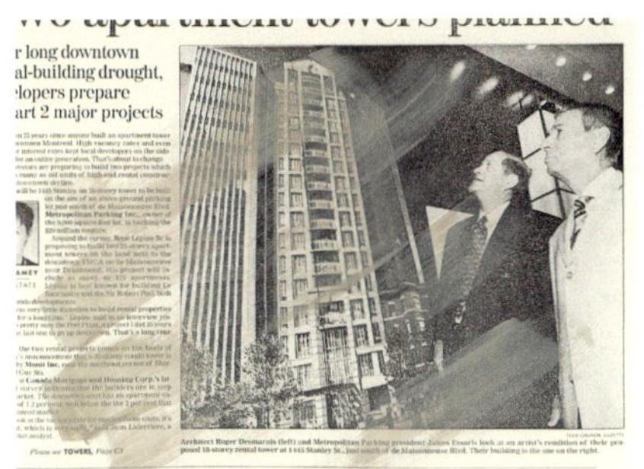
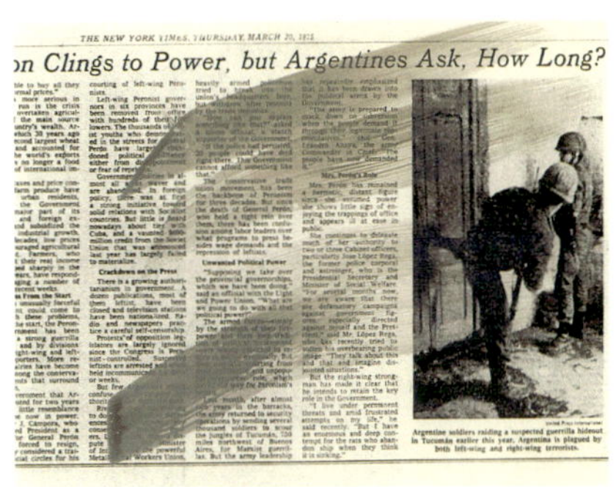
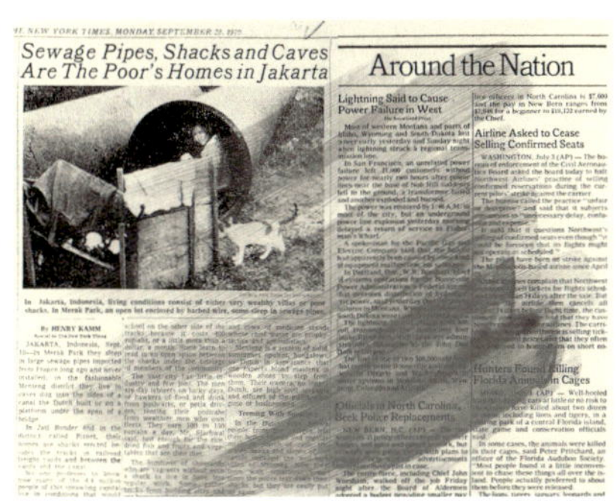
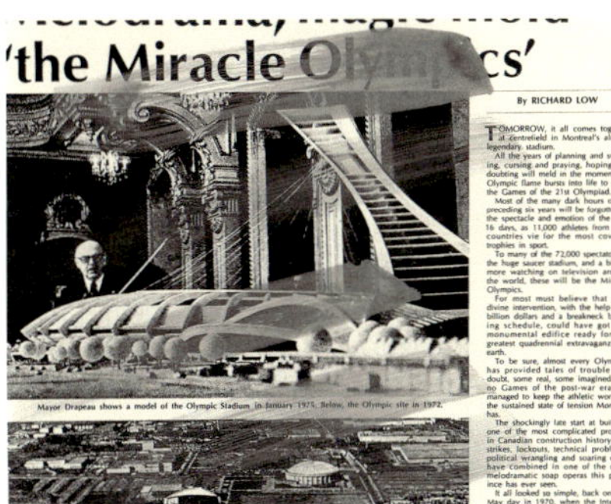
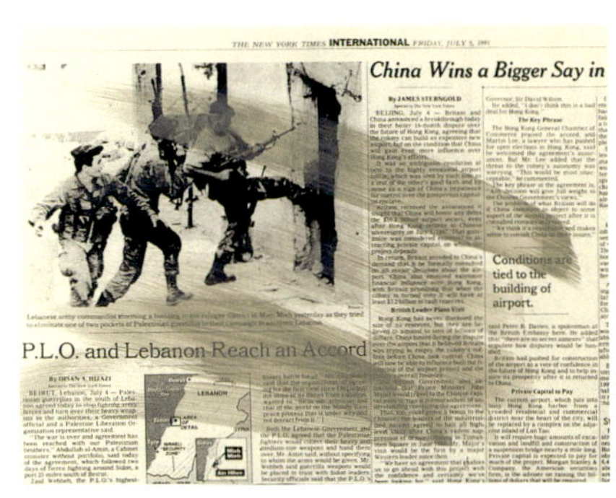
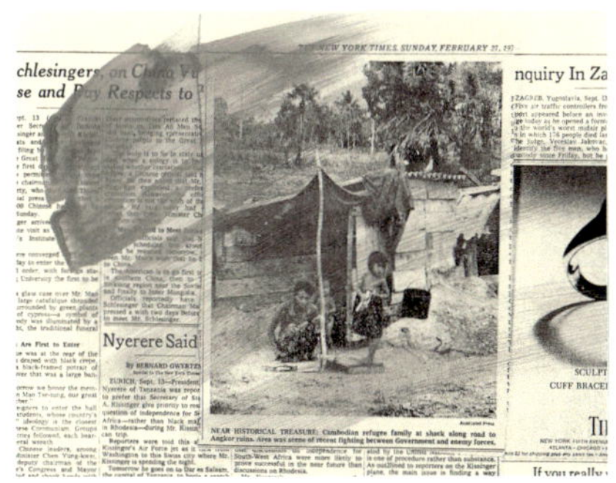
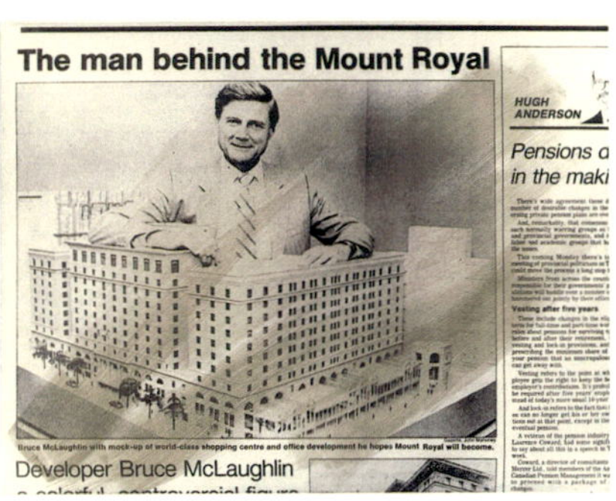
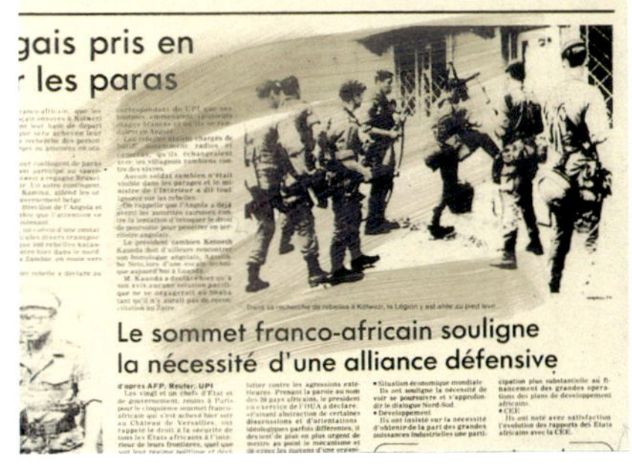
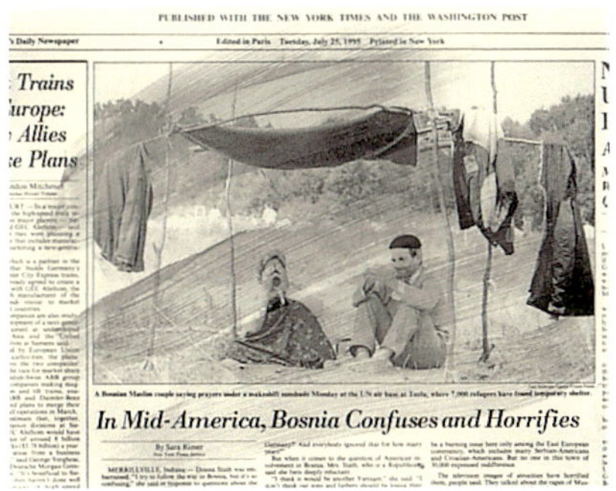

Series 20–29, *Meta-events: architecture*. Selected plates.

Series 30–39, *Fragmentation: doors, windows, walls and streets*. Selected plates.

Series 50–75, *Out on the edge: Adam's house, cities on the move, Noah's Ark*. Selected plates.

UN DICTIONNAIRE…, 1970–2001. 425 Plates, each with acrylic on silver gelatin prints on fiber paper of parts of newspapers, each 28 x 35 cm (11 x 13¾ in.) Collection: The Canadian Centre for Architecture, Montréal.

interaction between people and their constructed surroundings. Insofar as a series of images may constitute a coherent record of a discernible interaction, a record of common meaning, the classification assumes the character of a "dictionary," *UN DICTIONNAIRE*…. A dictionary is self-referential; words are defined by other words. Similarly, the images of *UN DICTIONNAIRE*… define one another, one image pushing at the visibility—the meaning—of another. A dictionary also traces the mutability of meaning. Emerging relationships are named, rendered visible— picking up on ideas of tacit knowledge where the *MEMO SERIES* left off.

Seen together, the diverse images of calamities, disasters, and celebrations fuse into a single all-embracing reality. One's focus shifts from the singularity of an event to its place in a field of evolving relationships between people and built things. One is no longer certain whether buildings and cities are going up or coming down. What is certain is a sense of pervasive tur- moil. Even the benign models of buildings and cities in the hands of their progenitors, *SERIES 20–29*, seem to evoke the struggle inherent in the accumulation of capital and social order that is required to marshal the resources needed to transform models into buildings.

The current version of *UN DICTIONNAIRE*… consists of 428 plates organized in a sequence of forty-six series and nine themes. Each plate reproduces, photographically, a slice of a news- paper page. The initial series, *SERIES 0.1–0.9*, introduce the capacity of events to propel buildings and cities into our consciousness. In *SERIES 1–9*, bombings, earthquakes, fires, and floods lay bare the fragility of buildings and cities reduced to ruins and rubble. *SERIES 10–19* gather images showing surfaces of buildings and cities peeled away to reveal undifferentiated frames and grids, the structure of structures. *SERIES 20–29* concentrate on models of buildings and cities in the hands of people in power; the degree of control they exercise appears inversely related to the size of the models. *SERIES 30–39* highlight mechanisms of societal control where men in uniform target our gaze at mere details, the doors and windows that attract their feet and fists, so that one does not get the whole picture. *SERIES 40–49* allow a glimmer of a world of exclusion where people are in physical contact with their constructed surroundings but are trapped in the minutiae of their existence, often reduced to vague blurs suspended in a hiatus of time and place. *SERIES 50–59* and *SERIES 60–69* gather images of people thrashing about on the fringes of society where "sacred" and even "sublime" constructs appear in a cruel replay of deeply rooted human impulses, as if Adam is still struggling to rebuild a house in Paradise. *SERIES 70–79* presage a world where overpopulated cities cruise the face of the earth like so many Noah's Arks. Finally, *SERIES 100* presents a replay of all previous themes as seen in images of the destruction of the World Trade Center, New York, in September 2001.

YS Our world is saturated with images. How do you go about selecting those images that you include and those that you set aside or even discard? How do you select the most iconic images, the ones that best describe your intentions? The selection process would seem to be a central issue in your work, since most of your photo-paintings are based on, or derived from, your *UN DICTIONNARE*… archive.

MC Certain photo images seem to speak directly to my hands. Some murmur away that they need a line here, others lust for a stroke of color there, particularly matte prints or high-contrast photocopies that ache to receive the caress of some smooth graphite! Lines drawn on a photo- graph open the image, extracting the layers of an extended landscape, enticing you to get in and walk around.

 YS At some point in your work you began to paint over photographs that you took yourself...

MC In the 1970s I went through a concentrated period of photographing buildings in various regions of Québec. What emerged are carefully wrought images conveying the formal, often heroic character of ordinary buildings. A few of these images led later to photo-paintings, for example *Parable No. 3... La Prairie* (1990). This interest in the buildings of Québec culminated with *Les Maisons de la rue Sherbrooke* (1976), followed by a series entitled *Front Page Constructions* (1978–79) in which Suprematist figures and De Stijl planes are extracted from the front pages of the business sections of newspapers.

Two images from Trois-Rivières, Québec, were crucial to my subsequent development of photo-paintings. The first image was appropriated from a 1974 government publication announcing federal funding for the "urban renewal" of a workers' *quartier* in Trois-Rivières at a time when urban renewal meant urban removal. The image of a shabby house was, for me, a striking presence, its simple volume evoking the outline of a classical temple. The traditional orientation of a house on a street was turned ninety degrees so that its *"mitoyenne"* (party) wall was facing the street, like a monumental frontal plane in the manner of a Baroque facade; within this plane the frame of a door and a window cut out a Latin cross. This house embodied heroic evocations while exuding obvious signs of poverty. It was no more than a converted garage; the walls were thin, the materials meager. The imminent demolition of the house accentuated the fragile existence of its inhabitants, living in the shadow of a factory and trapped in the grip of an authoritarian Church. At the confluence of a trinity of rivers, people built a house evoking both a temple and a tomb where they lived to expunge their fate.

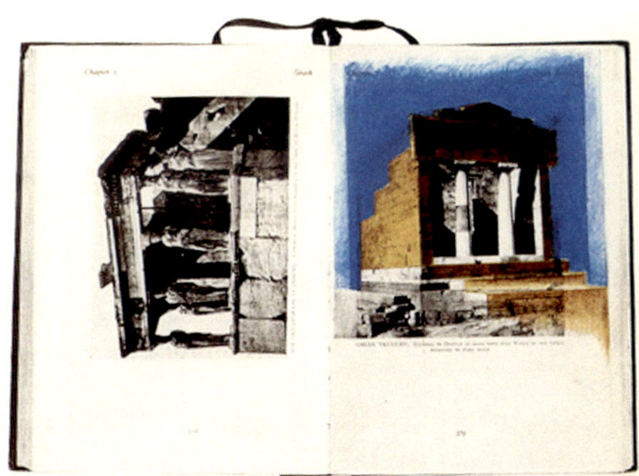

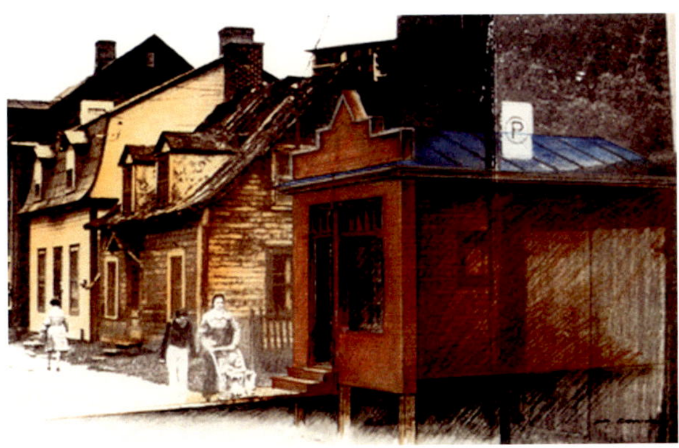

Chapitre deux... un monument à Trois-Rivières, 1975–77. Colored pencil and wax crayon on black-and-white photograph, 41 x 51 cm (41⅛ x 20 in.). Collection: The National Gallery of Canada, Ottawa.

Une histoire... le trésor de Trois-Rivières, 1975. Colored pencil and wax crayon on black-and-white photograph, 40.5 x 62 cm (16 x 24½ in.). Collection: The National Gallery of Canada, Ottawa.

Le Trésor de Trois-Rivières, 1975. Wood construction, 390 x 290 x 410 cm (153½ x 114⅛ x 161⅜ in.). Collection: The National Gallery of Canada, Ottawa.

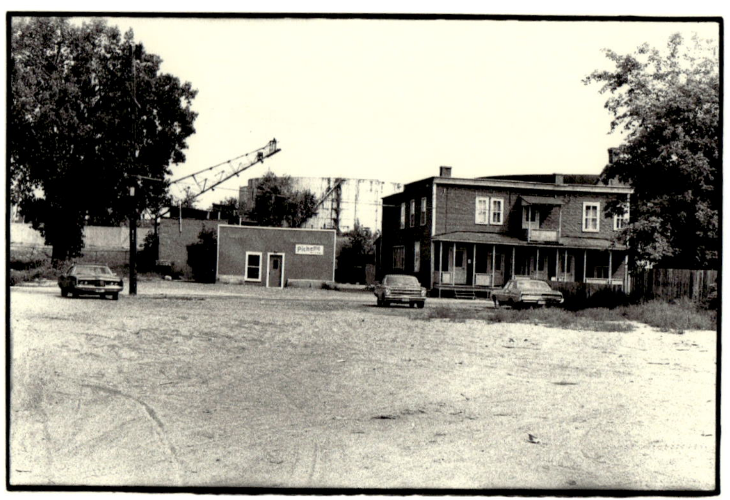

If one is to go by reference books, this small house has no history. The first thing I did was paint an image of the house onto an illustration of a Greek temple with similar proportions in a book called *The World's Greatest Monuments*. Then, onto a photograph of this house I superimposed a portrait of the house. This portrait then served as the basis for a third action, the reconstruction of a full-size version of the house recast as a sphinx to emphasize its enigmatic content.

The second Trois-Rivières image—the significance of which revealed itself slowly over a two-year period—was a 1975 photograph of three ordinary structures, each picking up on facets of contemporary archetypes: a wood-box building resembling an embodiment of Vitruvius's "primitive hut;" a wood tenement reeking of the urban history still haunting cities in Québec; and a cylindrical reservoir of a nearby factory invoking ideal geometry as a force of nature. The photo-paintings that ensued focused the metaphoric content of these currents (plate Nos. 7 and 8, pages 54–55).

The photo-paintings evolved; there was no turning back. What at first seemed to be a marginal "hinge" activity brought together two major concerns in my work: a constant impulse to transform my surroundings into photographs, along with the necessary transposition of an existing locale onto a set of manipulable images so that it could assume the characteristics of a "site," a place to build on; and an equally constant desire to construct, to physically assemble, materials on a given "site."

If, in a photo-painting, figure and ground are interchangeable, then the transposition of a figure of a place into a building site becomes the ground for the figure of a construction-installation. In some cases, the photograph of a construction-installation became the "site" since many of the construction-installations were purposely temporary. Subsequent photographs of these temporary constructions would serve as the basis of painted images—the after-life, the reincarnation of temporary pieces—for instance, *Room 202, P.S.1* (1979.) A series of temporary and site-specific works followed, including *A Chicago Construction* (1982), *A Toronto Construction* (1982), and *A Kingston Construction* (1983), each composed of mirror-image portraits of their emplacements. This phase of work came to fruition with a 1992 commission for the inaugural exhibition of the Musée d'art contemporain de Montréal. The resulting artwork—*Parabole no 9...ainsi soit-il: les usines ferment, les musées ouvrent* (1992)—consisted of two large-scale photo-paintings out of which stepped constructed, "site-specific" figures. As a young friend mentioned, it was as if "something broke out of the painting and walked across the room." By the 1980s what began as superimposed drawings and paintings on images of "sites" became autonomous works in themselves. I began painting over photographs that I had been taking since the late 1960s, particularly those photographs that evoked ready-made counter-images that were just waiting to spring out of the emulsion of an enlarged print.

The primary source of images that dominated the photo-paintings, however, was the *UN DICTIONNAIRE...* archive. The edgy tabloid news images involving aircraft from the *MEMO SERIES* evolved into *IN FLIGHT...* (1990–94), a series of pastel paintings on photographs of airplane crashes. *IN FLIGHT...* responded to a questioning of the faith people had in technology,

Pichette Nettoyeur, Trois-Rivières, 1975. Gelatin silver print on fiber paper, 27.8 x 35.3 cm (11 x 13⅞ in.). Collection: Canadian Museum of Contemporary Photography, Ottawa.

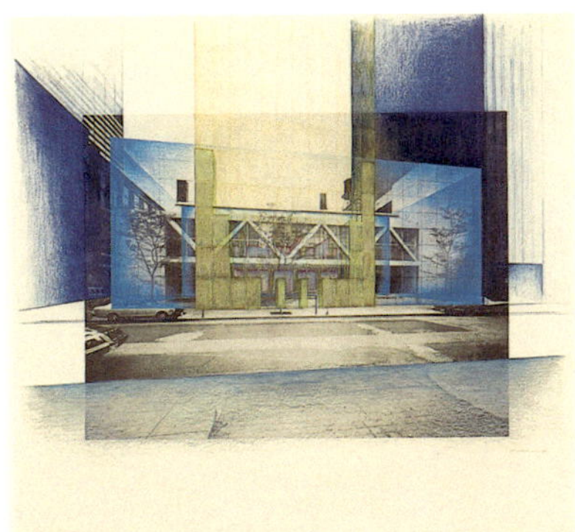

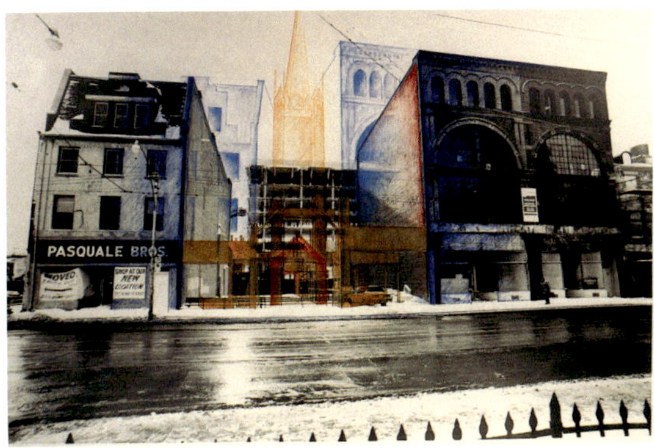

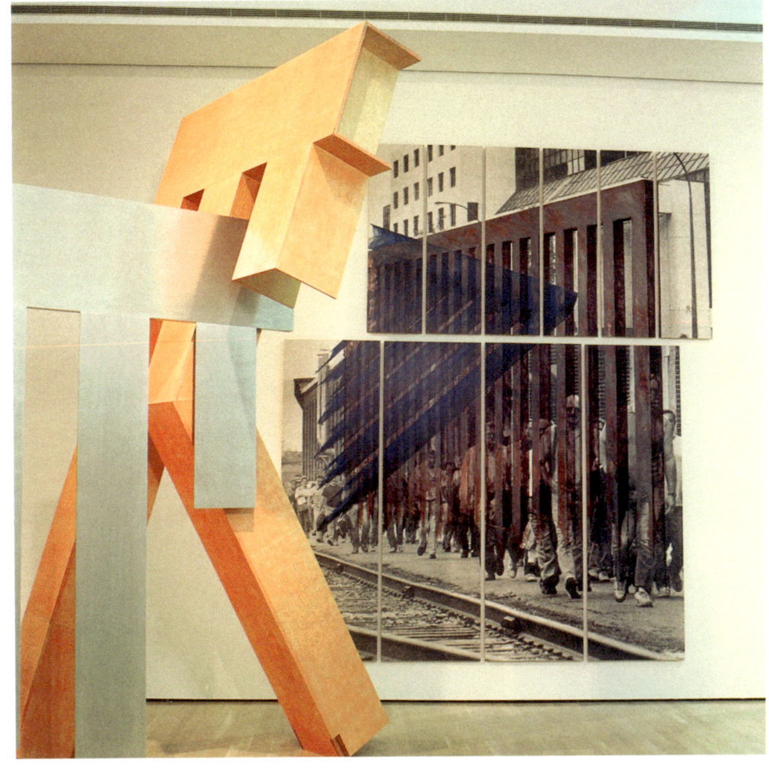

Chicago Construction, No 1, 1981. Colored pencil and wax on black-and-white Photostat copy from screened photograph, 62.9 x 66 cm (24¾ x 26 in.). Collection: Art Gallery of Ontario, Toronto.

Toronto Construction, No. 4, 1982. Colored pencil and wax crayon on black-and-white screened photograph, 56 x 76 cm (22 x 30 in.). Collection: The National Gallery of Canada, Ottawa.

and hence the symbols whereby twentieth-century artists would signal their avant-garde status—for example, Suprematism with its airplanes in flight, Marcel Duchamp with his chessboard. In studies I had done while working on key photo-paintings in the early 1990's, Suprematism came to be denoted by the intersecting planes of the broken wings of crashed airplanes, Duchamp by a floating chess table—virtual parables. If *UN DICTIONNAIRE...* elucidated meaning within a proliferation of news images, the *PARABLES...* drew viewers into the totemic space of these images. The photographic surfaces became no more than transparent openings onto a world behind and before the camera. It is as if the surfaces of the photographs were activated, figural structures were detached, transformed, and superimposed onto the original surfaces to elucidate the content and the historical roots of the images. What become evident was an ongoing tension between contemporary idioms and past habits, between shifting "thresholds" of perception and the struggle to represent such elusive boundaries. [...]

YS The way you build an image of a painted photograph, the way you strip it down and go back and forth, how you blow up a photograph then wash it with some paint and draw an axonometric, a plan, or an elevation, you construct a very convincing social space that distinguishes your work. [...] What does the grey paint that you add in an almost casual manner to newspaper photos bring to the work? What happens when the original newspaper page becomes obscured?

MC Rather than obscuring the original, the painted layers highlight its substance. At first I presented (at P.S.1 Contemporary Art Center, New York, 1979) the photographic plates of *UN DICTIONNAIRE...* without a grey overlay and discovered that people were more attentive to the images if the surface of the photograph was "placed" inside itself—a hint of obscurity proved to be a necessary incentive to encourage people to look for substance in an image. [...] The grey wash was partially transparent, the random edges of the roughly applied brushstrokes left parts of text uncovered. Time has rendered these odd bits of text intriguing—I now find myself trying to complete unfinished sentences. Many viewers assume that the pieces of text were strategically left visible as clues to the content of the work and/or the artist's intentions.

Parabole no 9...ainsi soit-il: les usines ferment, les musées ouvrent (detail), 1992 (after a photograph of the closing of the Angus Shops Locomotive Works, Montréal, and a photograph of the new Musée d'art contemporain de Montréal, which appeared in Montréal's *Le Devoir* newspaper in 1991). Installation: wood (partially painted and vanished), lacquered aluminum, and acrylic paint on gelatin silver prints mounted on paper and on wood, 400 x 1220 x 410 cm (157½ x 480¼ x 161⅜ in.). Collection: Musée d'art contemporain de Montréal.

YS What about people who seem to be involved with real buildings in real time? The body does make its appearances in *UN DICTIONNAIRE…*, but it is codified with emptiness, negation, and the "marginal other."

MC It seems to me that all of *UN DICTIONNAIRE…* is about people who are "involved with real buildings in real time." Moreover, human figures appear in virtually all the plates, from people shifting through the debris of buildings, to people in power clasping mini-models of built reveries, to people in uniform forming lines in public, urban, open spaces. Let's look at *SERIES 44* as an example of people involved with real buildings. Here is a group of images focusing on people at the bottom of the social heap, the unprivileged in our societies for whom the built world has become a restrictive place of reduced space and confinement—*un monde concentrationnaire*. They inhabit a new world of corridors, "mean streets," where the marginal and the poor are obliged to wait, be it for a permit or for medical treatment, as if it were a punishment for their indigent condition.

Bodybuilding   BUILDING BODIES

YS There is a filmmaker, Dorothy Arzner, from the 1930s who made the film *Craig's Wife* about a house, or rather, a woman in a house. The house is not just a house, but also the film's protagonist. Over time Craig's wife (Harriet) becomes the house. She occupies it and rids it of the factors she detests—her husband, for instance. This film makes me think about Louise Bourgeois's commitments, and yours. There is a clear difference in the way you both convey and use architecture; nevertheless I sense a strong resonance between you two.

MC I grew up on a diet of art journals that my father would recycle from his various acquaintances and I was at least aware of Louise Bourgeois's existence when, in the early 1980s, I found in a basement bin of art oddities in a New York City bookstore a catalogue of a show of her work at the Max Hutchinson Gallery. Reproduced in the catalogue were several prints of her *Femme Maison* series (1947) that impressed me both in terms of her take on Freud and her manner of spontaneously sketching a fusion of animate and inanimate. I then came across a book published on the occasion of a 1995 exhibition of her drawings. From her *Femme Maison* prints, to the drawing *Les voleuses de gratte-ciel* (1949) and *The Accident* (1992), the resemblances to my work were evident, even though the reasons why were obscure. Louise Bourgeois would draw a body as if it were a house, whereas I would draw buildings as if they were bodies.

The metamorphosis of buildings into body parts evolved slowly in sketches over a number of years. The abandonment of American cities began to make the news by the mid 1970s. So, when in 1977 an image of President Jimmy Carter walking over the rubble of a city block in the South Bronx appeared in the wire services, it was quite simple to pick up the elements of a photo-painting (*Walking Stiffs… Strutting through the embers*, 1993). A row of abandoned buildings in the background of the image provided a key to the forms of the "building bodies," which led to the transformation of these figures into large-scale constructions in the 1992 Musée d'art contemporain de Montréal artwork. This preoccupation with "building bodies" came to a head with a 1997 invitation to do a public artwork in Hérouville-St-Clair, France.

A satellite town on the periphery of Caen, Hérouville-St-Clair, founded in the early 1960s, is an example of the 1920s tradition of German *Siedlungen* gone awry: a paradisiacal blend of buildings and gardens caught between bloated social intentions and weak material forms. There are no streets and no houses. People are set adrift on footpaths that lead them through a disparate mass of indistinguishable blocks floating in fields. Ironically, in this city conceived in the name of social democracy, there is no communal spatial substance.

The suggested location of the work was in a pivotal area called the "city center." What city center? Nothing was there; it was no more than a name printed on town maps and in public-relation brochures. These brochures also revealed several projects for the site. In 1988 a proposal from the mayor's office called for a 100-meter *"Tour Européenne"* composed of three dissimilar buildings sitting one on top of the other, each to be designed by a different architect. Obviously, the *Tour* could not be built and was replaced by an equally improbable proposal for a commercial center. The commercial center, a low-level mall tucked beneath a kite-like roof hovering over the site, was succeeded a few years later by the most recent of projects, an administrative building by Jean Nouvel that was to be buried in mounds of earth—to be lowered into uterine-like tumuli. History was thus undone from skyscraper to cave, to the origins of all building.

My proposal for an intervention at Hérouville-St-Clair focused on the absence of the public urban content and on the transient materiality of the city. The human body is taken to be a fundamental register; the movement of the body is taken to be the basic spatial generator of urban form. In other words, the work's point of departure comes from the people who can be seen passing through or stopping to chat with each other in the interstitial no-man's-land between buildings. These figures are made to reappear, larger than life, as stainless steel constructs composed of pieces of buildings walking away from or toward a site: *CITIES ON THE RUN...Tenements in Search of Streets* (1996–98) and *CITIES ON THE RUN...Blocks in Search of a City* (1997–98). The figures are conceived to be displaced from one location to another. In Hérouville-St-Clair the presumption is that mobile figures placed in urban situations are to be catalysts of the catalyst. There is no specific location for the work. The pieces are moved at intervals from one site to another to designate the emplacement of a public urban structure and to invoke the expectation of its realization. Critical sites are identified by use, by their demonstration of the characteristics of a street or a square or an intersection. This city is now inhabited by large, shiny steel figures that can only be accommodated outside buildings and in public spaces. Here are the mobile *golems* that have emerged from the muddy tumuli to create life in the city (plate Nos. 25–29, pages 70–71).

YS What occurs in both Louise Bourgeois's and your representations of architecture? What is most interesting to me is what you take away, the way you extract aspects of the image to create room in a form that, in turn, creates potential, creates a sort of life force. [...]

MC To create "a sort of life force." [...] I take it that you are referring to what I mentioned yesterday, about an epiphany I experienced a number of years ago while accompanying a person close to me, a journalist on assignment, to a meeting between representatives of a United Nations committee on aboriginal rights and Mohawk band councils and elders. The meeting took place in the Mohawk longhouse at Kahnawake, on the south shore of the St. Lawrence River across from Montréal. During the long wait for the meeting to begin, I was sitting with some Mohawk "warriors" who were to perform the ceremonial component of the gathering. The meeting got underway in the late afternoon with drumbeats, chants, and dancing from the warriors, while the women conducted business with the UN representatives. What a division of labor! Those veritable creators of life, who carry and gestate the species' eggs, were busily negotiating important matters while their dandified counterparts—the artists, feathered warriors—emulated birthing rituals, ritualizing "creation." [...]

In other words, from within a discipline the emulation of relationships between people and their manufactured world can only serve to idealize it, or serve up a third-hand vision of reality. Moreover, the unraveling of this twisted cultural heap is complicated by the off-putting discourse of the specialist. For example, at a time when ergonomic issues are critical, we live in a particularly ill-fitting world, where the perception most people have of their bodies is drowning in a surfeit of images. All the while, the gurus of official cant are busily purging architecture of its anthropomorphic baggage. [...] So, along with the classified ads, I now seem to find pertinent imagery in the back pages of newspapers. [...]

Visualize a newspaper page with a grid of sixty vignettes of female torsos encased in standardized, name-brand bras, all on sale! The photo-painting that ensued from this was the first of a series entitled *One Fit Sizes All...* Through overlays of images, the series examines the total standardization of the built world we inhabit, from J.N.L. Durand, who in the early nineteenth century established a set of compositional rules that could be applied to all buildings, to the present, with its potential for genetically modifying the human form via the morphing of the size, shape, and behavior of the human species, willing it to fit the spaces that technology is capable of providing. This starts with critical components of human reproduction, the preening of the males (plate Nos. 23 and 24, pages 68–69). [...]

On the back pages of local publications, such as New York's *Village Voice* or Montréal's *Voir*, grids of calling cards advertise the denizens of the sex trade. Arranged under such headings as "Bodyworks" are photographs of seductive females who are in fact "she-males," whatever that may be. *ONE FIT SIZES ALL/No. 6: Bodybuildings: Guys & Grids* (2000–03) is a photo-painting with an overlay depicting structural grids, all enclosed within armor-like sections of skin that seem to have been peeled away from various body parts. The suggestion of buildings with body-like wrappings parallels the work of artists who intuitively return to the human figure as a primary reference, particularly at times when there is no dominant aesthetic. Another work, *ONE FIT SIZES ALL/No. 3: Blobs on the Grid...* (2000–02) looks at the current rash of "blob" architecture, with its round, bulbous, and humanoid shapes. While the strength of the "blobs" is intuitive, its discourse is weak. It represents itself as computer-generated and with no traces of anthropomorphic references, as if there could be no-*body* in a building (plate No. 23, page 68; plate No. 27, page 70) other than a suggestion of the dismembered Classical Orders or the hint of a new species of creatures that can satisfy any "reproductive" urges of anyone in sight (plate No. 30, page 72). [...]

A recent work, *CITIES ON THE MOVE, The Swinging Burbs* (2003–06), is also painted on a grid of advertisements for "Bodywork she-males" looking for "action." The "action" they get is depicted

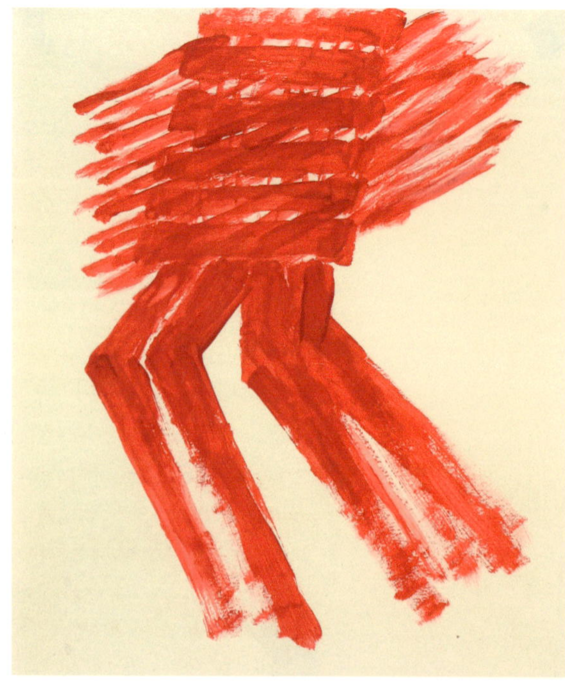

CITIES ON THE MOVE...My Architectones, No. 7, 2005. Gouache on archival paper, 43 x 35 cm (17 x 13⅜ in.). Collection of the artist.

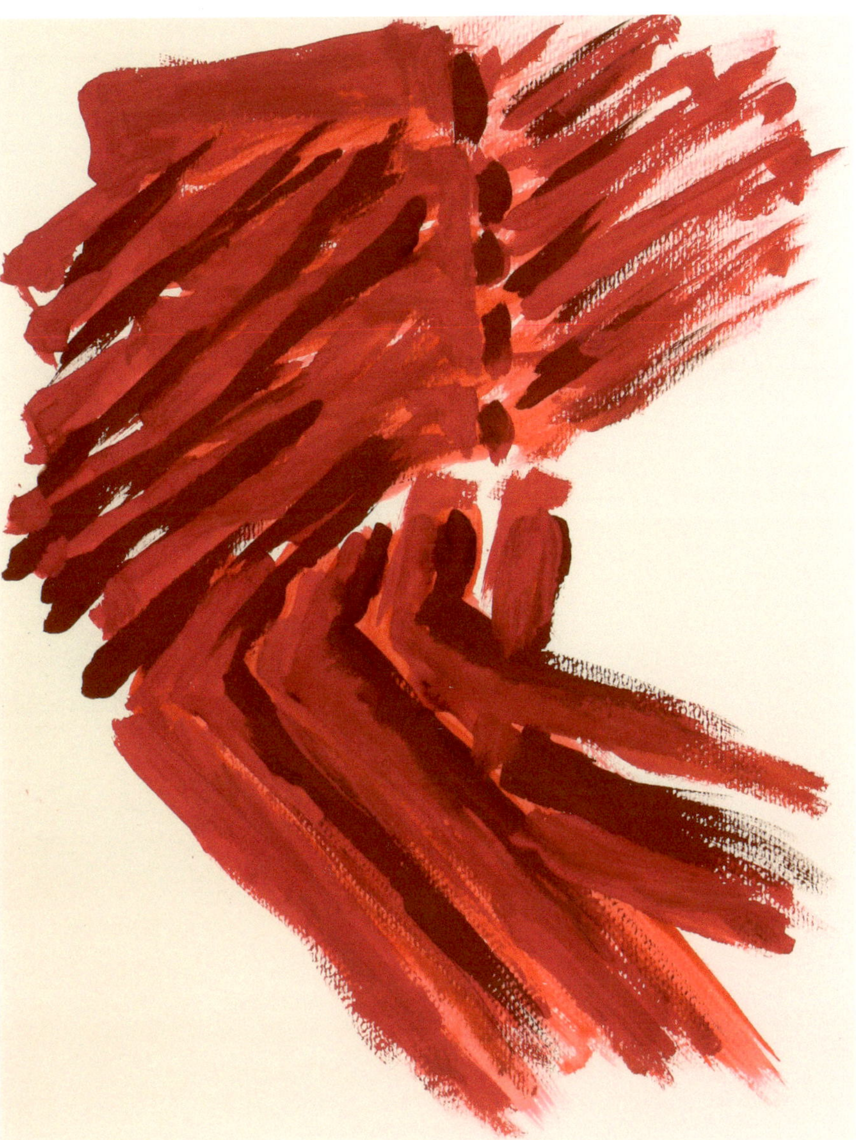

in the painted overlays that attempt to show things as they are. A "she-male" sensuality is con-
fronted by an equally seductive vision of a weekend visit to a local "burb." Recognizable media
images of "the good life" that can be enjoyed outside on the periphery of urban centers—a
country estate sheltered by trees, tailored lawns, a family, a husband, wife and children—linger
in the thoughts of the *paterfamilias* whose imagination dances with the sensuality of it all.
The actual greening of the male's existence is still conditioned by the *quartiers* of the city. [...]
Are these stories I tell myself once the day's work is done? Stories weave words, mere props,
the approximations of visual depictions (plate No. 31, page 73).

I am now working with images borrowed from swinger magazines, published prior to the
advent of Photoshop. The self-conscious narcissism apparent in these images is juxtaposed with
the collective narcissism evident in the figures of urban spaces such as city squares—for example,
the Piazza del Duomo in Milan—another long-time preoccupation of mine. I have also returned
to the *Femme Maison* prints and drawings of Louise Bourgeois—how she deals with the female
body. If a house is a receptacle and female, how could one treat the male body in a similar manner? A breakthrough for me came following a remark made by a female acquaintance. "Imagine,"
she said, "he wanted to put his thing into me!" I imagined my *RUNNING CITY* figures, the *golems*
with eight-foot lengths of two-by-fours standing out from their bodies, signifying the eternal
male drive to penetrate anything in sight in order to perpetuate the species. So here I am again
backing into edgy phenomena. [...]

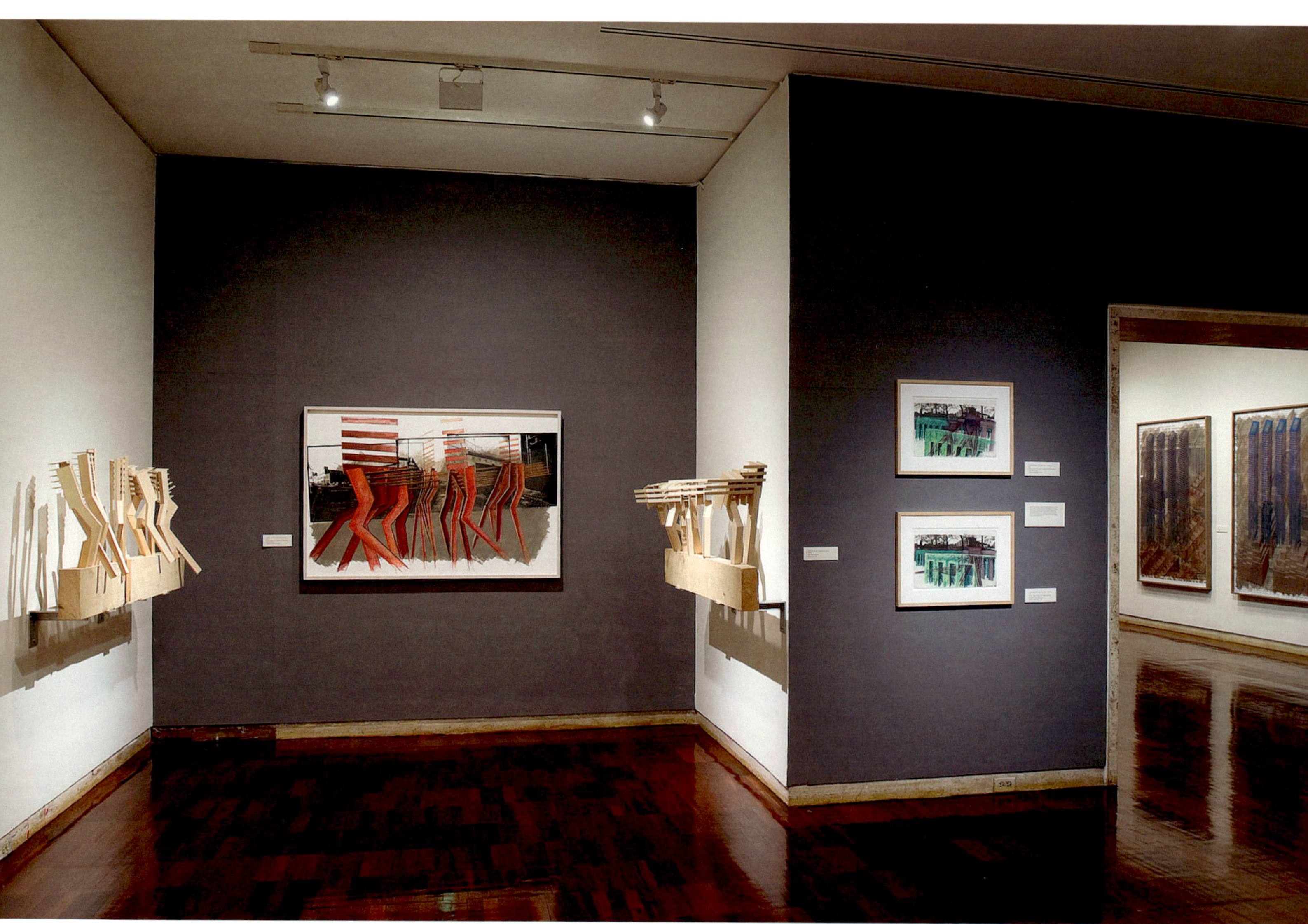

Between Observation and Intervention: The Painted Photographs of Melvin Charney, Americas Society, 2008. Installation view including the following artwork (from left to right): *CITIES ON THE RUN... Tenements on the Move*, 1996–98; *CITIES ON THE RUN... on the edges of industrial belts*, 2002–05; *CITIES ON THE RUN... Blocks Running Scared*, 1997–98; *Canada Memorial, Green Park, London... Study No. 7*, 1993; *Canada Memorial, Green Park, London... Study No. 8*, 1993; *THE AMERICAN CITY: Henry and Friends, Detroit, circa 1970*, 1996–97; and *THE AMERICAN CITY: Ieho Ming & Friends, Manhattan 1989*, 1999–2000. Photo: Arturo Sanchez.

Melvin Charney: The Art of Reformation, Redeployment, and Subversion

BY SAUL OSTROW

Over the past thirty-plus years, Melvin Charney's central focus as an artist has been to demonstrate how architecture and urban planning function as a system of control and societal exchange. In the book *Melvin Charney: Parcours de la Réinvention*,[1] with essays by Jean-François Chevrier, Johanne Lamoureux, and Jun Teshigawara, Charney's work received critical analysis within the framework of architecture and urbanism. Unlike in many of the art reviews of his work, in *Parcours* architecture and urbanism are pinpointed as playing a metaphorical role in his work rather than being the determinant subjects.

According to the texts included in *Parcours*, which are themselves analytically and theoretically grounded in Post-structuralism, Charney's goal is represented as being one of making transparent the attendant assumptions and histories that wend their way through architecture's representational regime. Consequently, while this essay should be read against the backdrop of the accompanying exhibition of painted photographs, it should also be read as a complement to the essays collected within *Parcours*. This is because I have not limited myself to the work in the exhibition, but address the general schema of the inner workings, or the aesthetic ecology, of Charney's practice. I have chosen to do so in order to articulate my suspicion that, for the most part, the default position from which Charney's narratives are interpreted, based largely on the notion that his work is characterized by architectural mutilation and improvisation, is a flawed one. This is because while such an interpretation may satisfactorily explain Charney's critique of urbanism, it does not lend itself readily to addressing the underlying aesthetic propositions, assumptions, and textual implications of the strategies, forms, and relationships that this critique employs.

As it is obvious that what Charney creates is not architecture in the traditional sense, we as viewers, in our desire to know or understand what he does create, emblematically interpret his work as being about ideas "about" architecture. In doing so Charney's practice, his works, and the very discourse on architecture itself are ripped from their foundations. This is the condition to which the reviews included in a typical press kit customarily submit. By converting (the discourse of) architecture into the substance of Charney's work, they effectively modify the signifier (the work of art) so that it may point toward some aspect of that singularity. What results from this initial act is the fact that all aspects of the artwork are then indexed to this doppelganger. By attaching the artwork to an over-determined signified, instead of achieving the desired effect of elucidating its meaning and bringing the work closer to our understanding, it is moved farther away from us and becomes embedded in the spectral realm of literal, instrumental, and institutional reasoning. Paradoxically, this is the realm I believe the artist/designer Charney means to critique by creating a signifier that fluctuates between signified and mark, between metaphor and material condition, between expectations and associations.

The failings of the standard interpretations therefore arise from the fact that they subordinate the signifier that Charney has constructed (in this instance the work of art) to an over-determined signified (understood to be a critique of architecture and urban planning). By reducing Charney's work to a problem that can be expounded upon, the opportunity to consider how the qualities of the signifier itself constitute yet another text is entirely lost. To imagine, as the standard interpretation does, that Charney simply *employs* architectural motifs to set into motion a critical discourse concerned with the incongruities of urban life, then one fails to recognize that the signifier's own disposition—its very construction—inhibits the conceit of the very narrative it appears to facilitate. I surmise that the intent of Charney's strategy of subversion is to forestall the habits by which the signified overrides all other considerations as to what else the content of the artwork may be. In other words while "architecture" may act as a motivation, the signifier (the work of art) as deployed by Charney is a self-referential reminder—and a remainder—that comes to exist, aesthetically, in an agonistic relation to its referent(s): in this case, architecture and urbanism. As such, the artwork both doubles and collapses its sign function.

By recursively turning in upon itself, Charney's works consequently perform the dual task of carrying a message (in the register of the signified) and making the signifier stand out, salient and visible, as a special type of signifier, one that is not singularly and unitarily assigned to a signified that would render it invisible by using it merely as a vehicle or carrier of content or intent. Within the unique terms by which Charney's artwork fulfills its task as signifier, it sets the work of art itself in contradistinction to this function of being a signifier, one that merely performs a referential function. Thus, Charney uses the work of art to fracture the classical dyad formed by signifier/signified. He does this by asserting for the artwork a recursive self-identity (an aesthetic) that differs from and remains profoundly non-identical to its function. This differentiation represents not *excess* but the *potential* of the signifier to be plural, multivalent, unbounded. Inversely it is with an awareness of this latent potential that Charney sets out to create art.

Having thus proposed that, within Charney's work, there is a dynamic of aesthetics and semiotics predicated upon the conflict between signifier and its sign function, I have set about turning my initial suspicions into the subject of this critical study. As irony would have it, at the time I was writing this essay on Charney, I was also researching the question of what constituted a Subject relative to the work that art does. Each of the books I consulted in my efforts to address this question contained texts that offered critical perspectives on the issues of image, narrative, aesthetics, criticality, representation, and functionality. These texts—written by Liam Gillick,[2] Alison and Peter Smithson,[3] Thomas McDonough,[4] Jacques Rancière,[5] Nicholas Bourriaud,[6] and John Rajchman,[7] among others—began, subversively, to fill the margins of my thinking about Charney's painted photographs, and eventually circumscribed them completely. With time these texts combined with Charney's works to form a hypertext around the question, "How do we come to understand those artworks that require us to believe both in the artificiality of their representation and in the self-reflexivity of their criticality?"

Answering this latter question again required me to correct the interpretive strategy by which Charney's practice as artist/designer is subsumed by the text of its referents—architecture and urbanism. To do this it was necessary for me to remove Charney's work from the context created by those accounts, which assign to it the over-simplified meaning of being merely an allegory of architecture. Entering into the work through its aesthetic, i.e., the way its formal elements are ordered, is to emphasize the economy of formalist/phenomenological/materialist effects that order the recursive identity of the artwork (as a sign) as a heterotopic space that accommodates and is inclusive of the differing references and associations that may be assigned to both signifier and signified. Consequently, by unlocking (or decrypting) the aesthetic strategies which all too often enforce the unity of signifier (to indicate) and signified (to reference), I sought to dislodge and expose the "reality" and the "truth" of the work of art as articulated by Charney.

By reversing the illusory presences and absences created by the relationship of object and subject to site, style, structure, form, materiality, presentation, etc., the deep structures and the central values that guide Charney are thrown into relief. For instance this inversion challenges the presumption that, because he chooses to use architectural imagery of a certain type, he intends to signify narratives concerning the condition of architecture, and not that of sculpture. However, this in turn would allow us to understand that the assertion that his work is "about" architecture and urban planning does not necessarily preclude the possibility that it might be also be "concerned" with sculpture's relation to architecture. Yet, in this context we would have to distinguish Charney's concerns from those of the sculptor/architect Tony Smith, who, by inversely focusing on the formal function of scale as an aesthetic experience common to both architecture and large-scale sculpture, could assert that the unfinished New Jersey Turnpike was sculpture. It is this affinity between architectural form and scale that also informs the pseudo-architectural projects of Michael Heizer's *Complex One*. However, due to the specificity of their conception of sculpture as a functionless object, in order for such projects to qualify as sculpture, they must negate the complex of programs, systems, and networks by which architecture materially organizes and signifies social, cultural, and political conditions and relationships. As such, beyond the reference to architectural form, there is no conceptual correspondence between the types of large sculptural projects mentioned here and Charney's work.

Likewise, because it can be said with some confidence that Charney is concerned with architecture as a system of signification rather than as an object, then it may seem logical to draw parallels between his work and the principles that guide Gordon Matta-Clark's urban interventions (such as cutting through a building) or the site-specific subversions of Michael Asher. (I am referring specifically to those situations in which Asher removes windows or walls, or in some other manner modifies the architecture of the site of his exhibitions, as part of the exhibition itself.) Yet, again, despite the aesthetic strategies they may share, Charney differs from both these artists in that Matta-Clark and Asher are committed to producing either a situated object (in Matta-Clark's case) or a non-object (in Asher's) that serves as a medium through which the surplus narratives of their respective sites are activated.

If a conceptual and aesthetic model comparable to Charney's is to be found, it is in Robert Smithson's non-sites. Though Smithson does not deal with architectural imagery, his signifiers—geology, rocks, containers, maps, and text—intentionally refer back to an actual site that is unavailable to the viewer at the moment of his or her encounter with them, and at the same time constitute the very site of their signification. Charney redeploys this notion of the non-site (literally a "nowhere") to create the conditions under which architecture and art's imminent chain of potential signified meanings is not immediately deferred. It is in this retention, or conservation, of interpretative possibilities that one finds concrete evidence of Charney's aesthetic of absences, presences, and reinsertions. For instance, by recycling and recontextualizing the vocabulary of architecture, Charney forms a font of new images—which, paradigmatically, he employs to indicate architecture's own multifarious identity while, in the same instance, the resulting assemblages dispense with architecture as a trope. As such he replicates Smithson's logic, but to very different ends.

The suturing together of various deictic moments and antitheses form within Charney's work a recursive and self-reflexive content that delineates what the signifier (artwork) is and what its referents may be. Within this heterogeneous economy, in which the artwork is always asserting itself as a fact, what it may signify comes to be identified as something "other."

Subsequently, correspondences and associations become tentative. For instance in articulating an empty space between buildings, one might assume that they are meant to think that "disregard" is also being signified. Similarly, by presenting a facade independent of the building it purports to front, one may interpret this to be an act of deception, or associate the defacement of a photograph with a vision of vandalism.

Likewise, the incompleteness and fragmentary nature of Charney's installations symbolize transience, as do romantic follies, but also identify the persistent aspects of our built environment. These sites exist self-contradictorily as the signifier of a state of incompletion: even though we know they will never be complete, they are, in a sense, already complete as signifiers. Yet these acts respectively might also be seen as representing a breach, truthfulness, an intercession. The tension created by this multiplicity and alterity is surrendered when, in the name of making the complexity of the work intelligible, all its attributes are made subordinate to keywords which, in the case of the artist/designer Charney, have come to be architecture or urbanism.

This alternation between signifier and thing, this stutter, and the hesitancy it induces result in a pregnant moment that makes visible the patterns of thought *deployed* but not necessarily *employed. Obviously, this array of unstated, unseen, and unobserved logics are not limited to explicative narratives concerning architecture or urbanism, but appear in the same way that ideas, experiences, and things are physically and psychologically mapped onto the "reality" of our world.* The need to meditate upon these distinct and often conflicting states (both real and imagined) is used to provoke the viewer into extrapolating from and completing the work in his or her imagination. *This act of completion is in itself a signifier, in the sense that it signifies performatively the normally unconsidered, or un-noticed, cognitive processes that precede the interpretative act by which we explain and expand upon the conclusions that are drawn.*

As if to underline the point that Charney has set for the viewer the task of differentiating between what is encoded within his work and what may be projected onto its surfaces, his painted photographs re-enact this scenario in reverse. In these works he demonstrates how two images that occupy the same surface may misalign and, in so doing, create an illusory economy between them. In these works, which appropriate the conventional format of painting, Charney paints or draws squares and rectangles, strokes, architectural forms, and the occasional domestic object onto a foundation of photographic images taken from a variety of sources, including photographs that he himself has taken.

The geometry and style of the invented images evoke a hybrid of the expressionism of Russian Cubo-Futurism and the formalism of Constructivism. Within the painted photographs the perspective of the painted or drawn image literally shatters the illusionistic space of the photograph. Yet the quality of the paint or oil pastel applied over the photograph is often wholly or partly transparent or translucent. As if they were shadows cast upon shadows, these disembodied configurations form ghost-like presences that coyly accommodate key bits of the degraded photographic image beneath. Unlike these ghost-like images, the photographic images in their infinite variety signify the endless stream of images produced, reproduced, and distributed as so many consumable items are—a category to which these works may be added. As such, by doubling back onto themselves, the works acquire an aspect of their own subject. By jeopardizing themselves in this manner, they identify the point where the fields of art and mass media intersect, as well as the point where the future meets the past, and the role these interactions play within the framework of everyday life.

Often accompanied by a caption (in the sense that many of them derive from newspaper clippings), the photographic imagery forms a submerged archive of business mergers, governmental decisions, economic trends, and death; of the seedy, the perverse, the glamorous, and the exotically bizarre. When images from newspapers or advertisements are enlarged, their halftone or Ben-Day dot patterns are consequently magnified. This disfigurement through the crude act of using photography to mechanically reproduce itself as its own simulacra disengages and subverts the course of its reproduction. It disenfranchises its products from their claim of being an "image of" some absent reality, because its condition is now that of the real. Thus, in pitting the textual indeterminacy of the photographic image against the experiential specificity and apparent inventiveness of the painted image, the conventional expectations associated with each medium displace the narrative content that each is meant to deliver.

In the photo-works Charney exploits the desire to privilege the photographic image, even when it has been re-faced, and titillates the viewer with the promise of fulfilling those desires, namely to give body to the absences that are evoked and, by doing so, explain all. On the other hand, as with his assemblages of fragmented architectural motifs, we know that the comprehension promised will never be obtained through these photographs, because what they promise is already present in their very condition. Therefore, attempts on the part of the viewer to undo what Charney has done by recuperating the photographic image only reinforces the gap that exists between the material signifier and its dematerialized signified.

By not prescribing or implying any specific hierarchy for—or interpretation of—the coexistence of photographic and painted images on the same surface, Charney leaves the viewer to deal with an economy that only self-referentially speaks of erasure, concealment, and cancellation. Within their repetition of format and variety of imagery, each of the painted photographs operates in the same manner, elucidating the process by which signifiers summon up the indeterminacy of the imagined by promising to create a symbolic order. The casual displacement of means initiates the critical discourse as to the nature of art's function as both material and sign. Through this arbitration both the text of the signifier and the function of art are materially unfolded, making palpable and intelligible their participation in the theater of representation.

By engaging both openly and clandestinely in a critique of self (the signifier) and its other (its referents) via the surrogacy of the work of art, Charney positions his aesthetics as a social medium and, therefore, an ideological and political one. If we were to plot this position in a Venn diagram, it would occupy the space created by the overlapping territories of the Russian Productivists and Situationists. This brings to bear onto Charney's work two disparate and seemingly contradictory historical references: the latter represents the apex of Apollinarian rationalism and the former Dionysian revelry. I do so because, embedded in the respective visions of each movement, there is faith in the notion that aesthetics is not separate from everyday life but is in fact embedded into its fabric via the objects we possess, the things we look at, and the environment we inhabit. As such, Charney, in a manner similar to the Productivists and the Situationists (both of whose ideas he stylistically quotes and strategically appropriates), understands aesthetics as a system of values, criteria, and standards that create a worldview—that is, a unified structure through which all social systems are connected and as such may be used to reorganize our understanding of the self and of the world

In taking up the task of abolishing the boundaries between the fictional (hypothetical situations) and the real (material conditions), which circumscribe everyday life, the trinity of intervention, mediation, and re-evaluation thus forms the foundation for Charney's agenda of reformation, subversion, and redeployment, as it had done for the Productivists and Situationists. Guided by such principles, in using "images of architecture and photography," he not only generates critical commentary, observation, and protest, but also articulates optimistically a rhetorical proposition as to how the nonlinear, indeterminate, and self-referential texts of the visual signifier (the work of art) open up a space from which the deceitful may be deflected, and by which, in an instrumental manner, an over-determined signified can order our consciousness and being. The inference to be drawn as this proposition turns back upon itself is that, an explanation of why things happen, or how they may be impeded, does not lie within the domain of the function of art. Rather, part of art's function is to reveal the ways in which events and ideas resonate within one another, and in everyday life, and how they can be shown and acted upon by indirect means—such as that of the work of art. All else lies in the domain of the human being.

[1] J.-F. Chevrier *et al.*: *Melvin Charney: Parcours de la Réinvention* (Caen: Frac Basse-Normandie, 1998).

[2] L. Gillick: *Proxemics Selected Essays, 1988–2006* (Zürich: JRP/Ringer, 2007).

[3] A. Smithson and P. Smithson: "Capital City Berlin, Competition entry 1958, third prize," in C. Lichtenstein and T. Schregenberger, eds.: *As found: the discovery of the ordinary* (New York: Springer, 2001), pp.146–52.

[4] T. McDonough: "Ideology and the Situationist Utopia," in *ibid.*, ed.: *Guy Debord and the Situationist International: Texts and Documents* (Cambridge: MIT Press, 2004), pg.ix.

[5] J. Rancière: *The Future of the Image* (London: Verso, 2007), pg.91.

[6] N. Bourriaud: *Relational Aesthetics* (Dijon: les presses du réel, 2002), pp.41–48.

[7] J. Rajchman: *What's New in Architecture: Philosophical Events: Essays of the '80s* (New York: Columbia University Press, 1991), pg.152.

PLATES

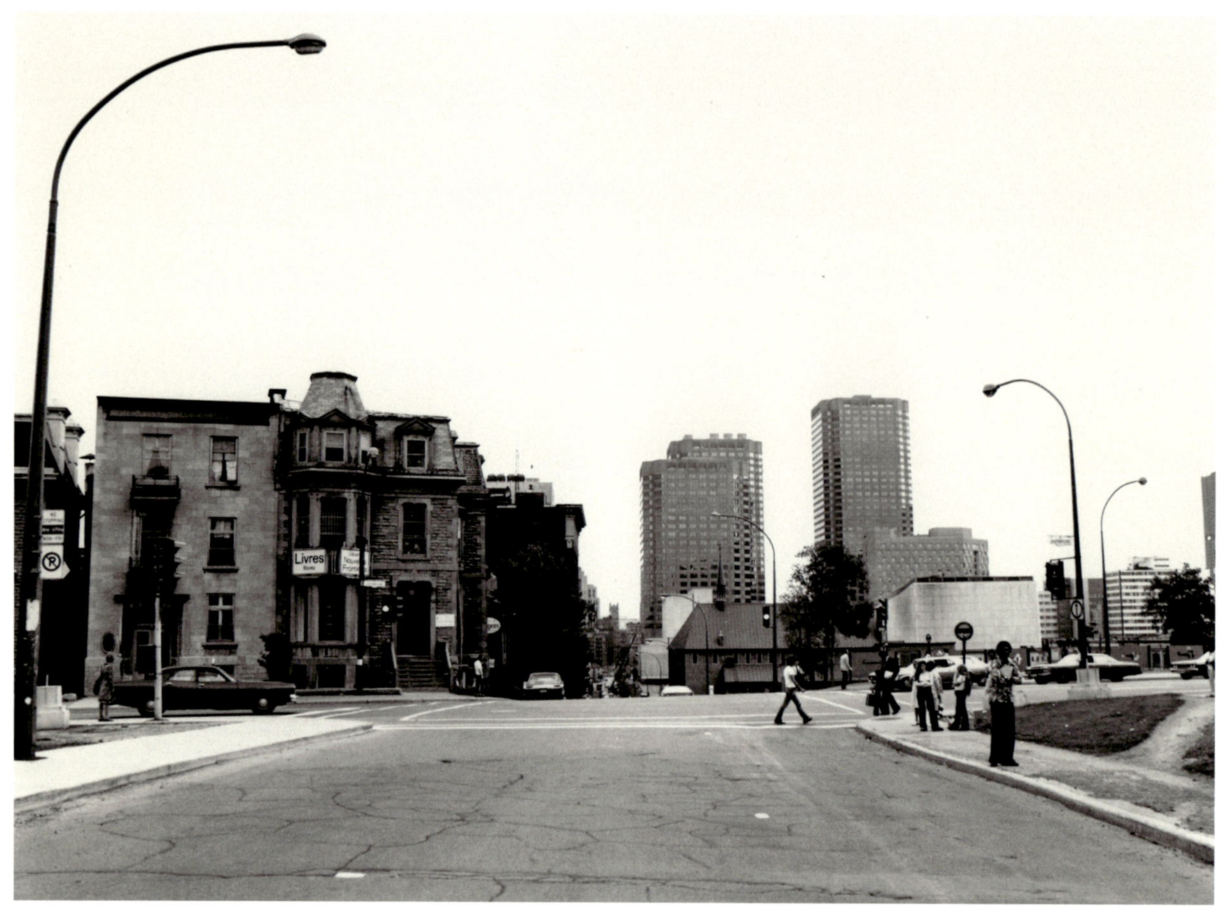

1   *THE SITE... Les Maisons de la rue* 1976

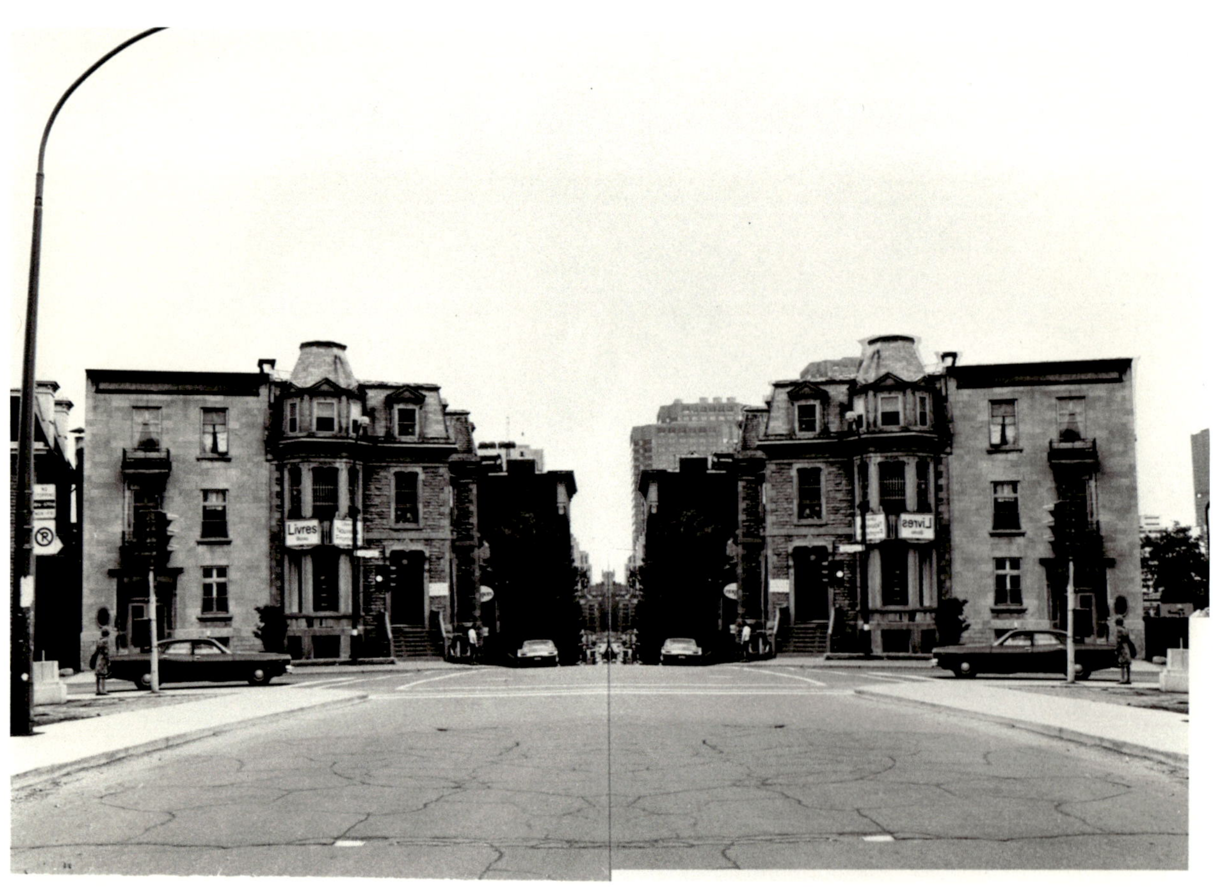

2   *THE SITE ALTERED... Les Maisons de la rue* 1976

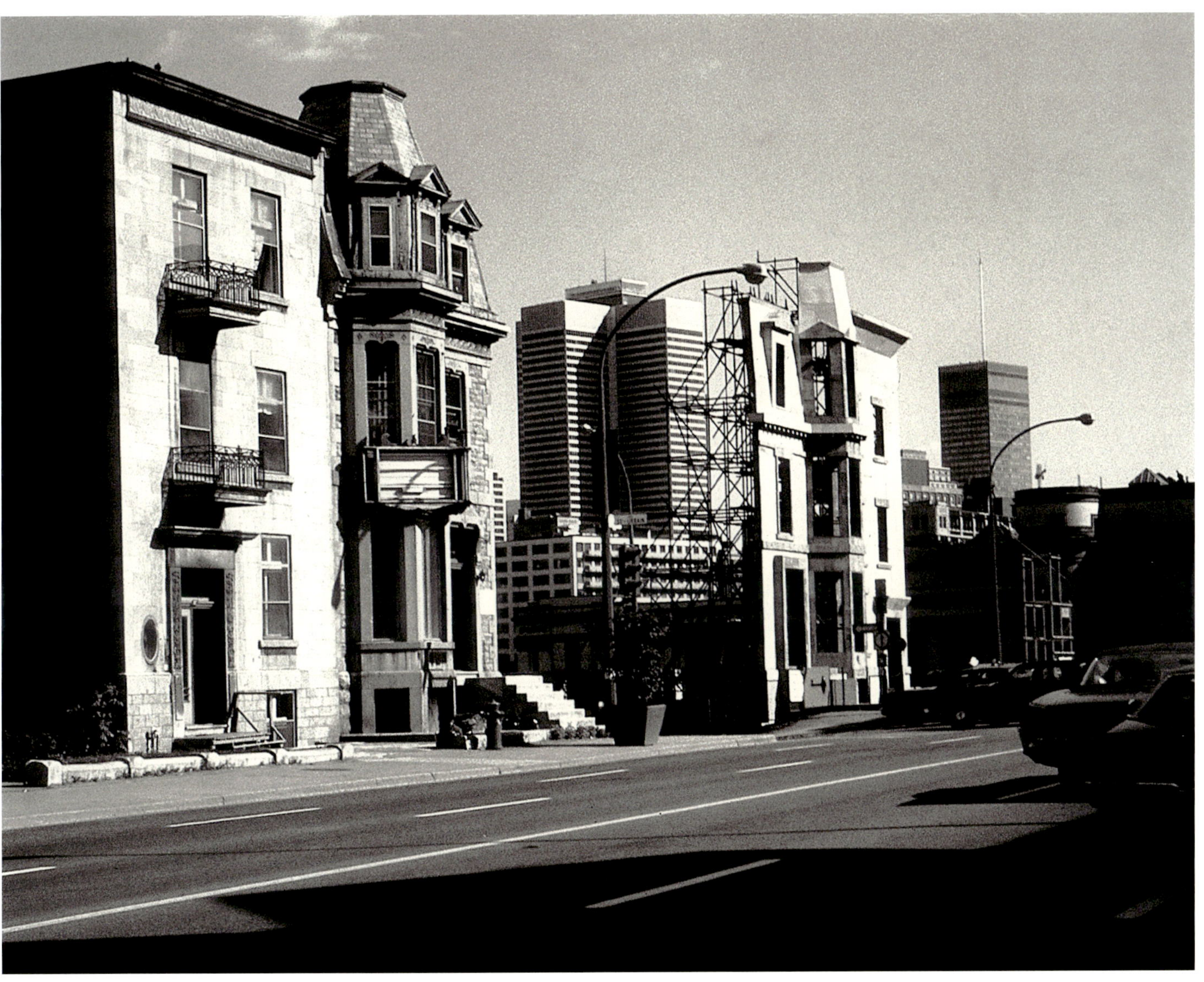

Les Maisons de la rue Sherbrooke 1976. Wood, steel, and concrete construction. 51 x 54 x 48 ft. Installation, Sherbrooke Street and Saint-Urbain, Montréal, Canada, June–July 1976. Commissioned by the Arts and Culture Program of the XXI Olympiad.

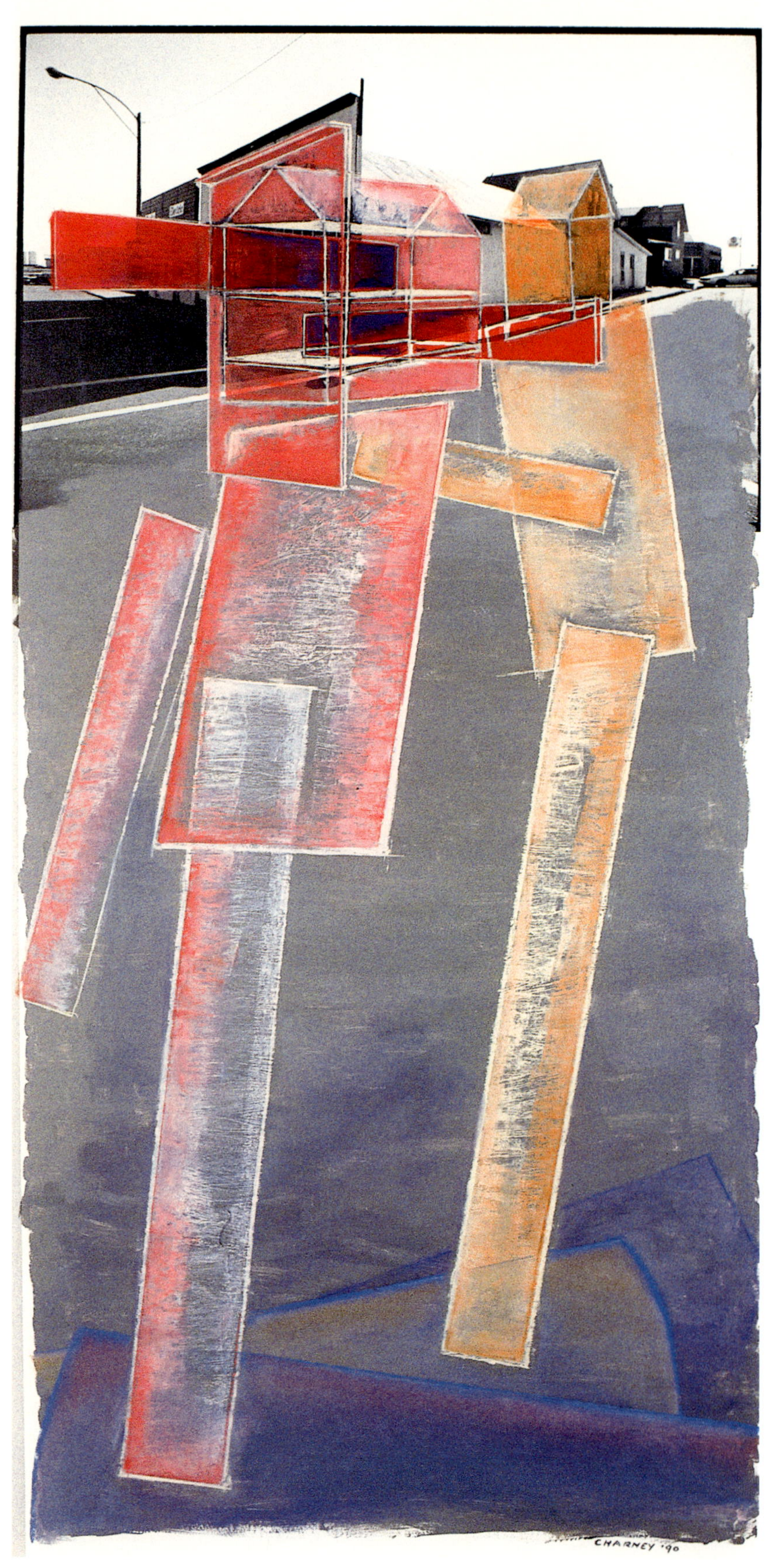

4   *In Flight... de Stijl as a Prairie Dog* 1990

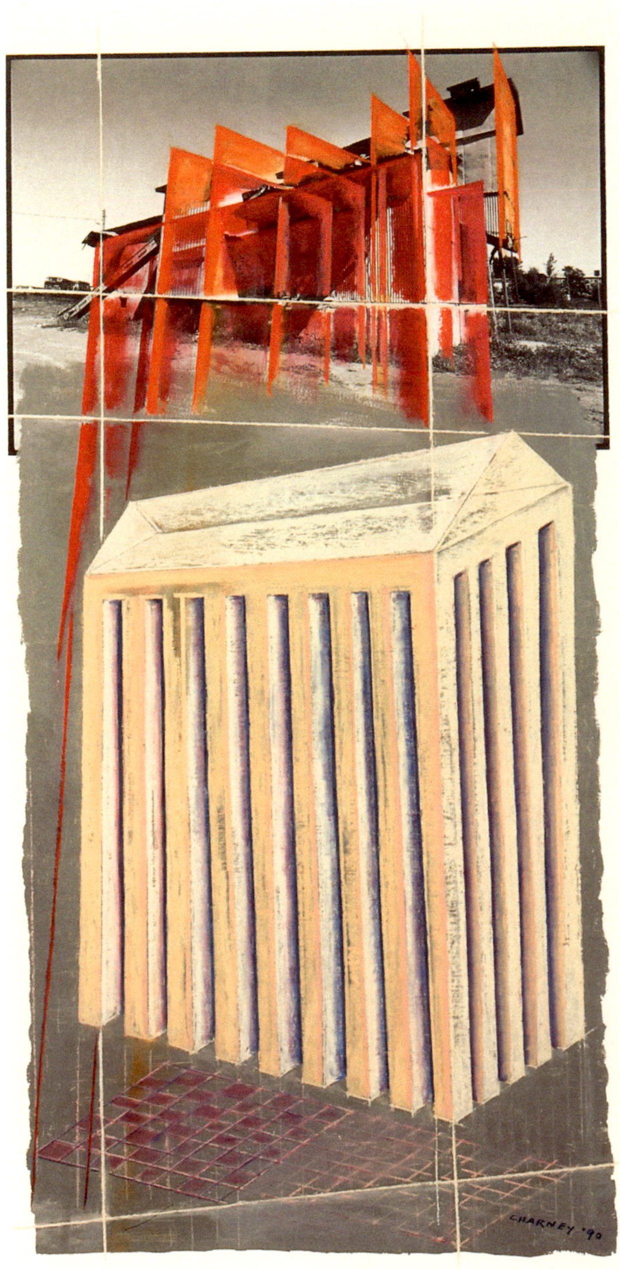

5   *Parable No. 3... La Prairie* 1990

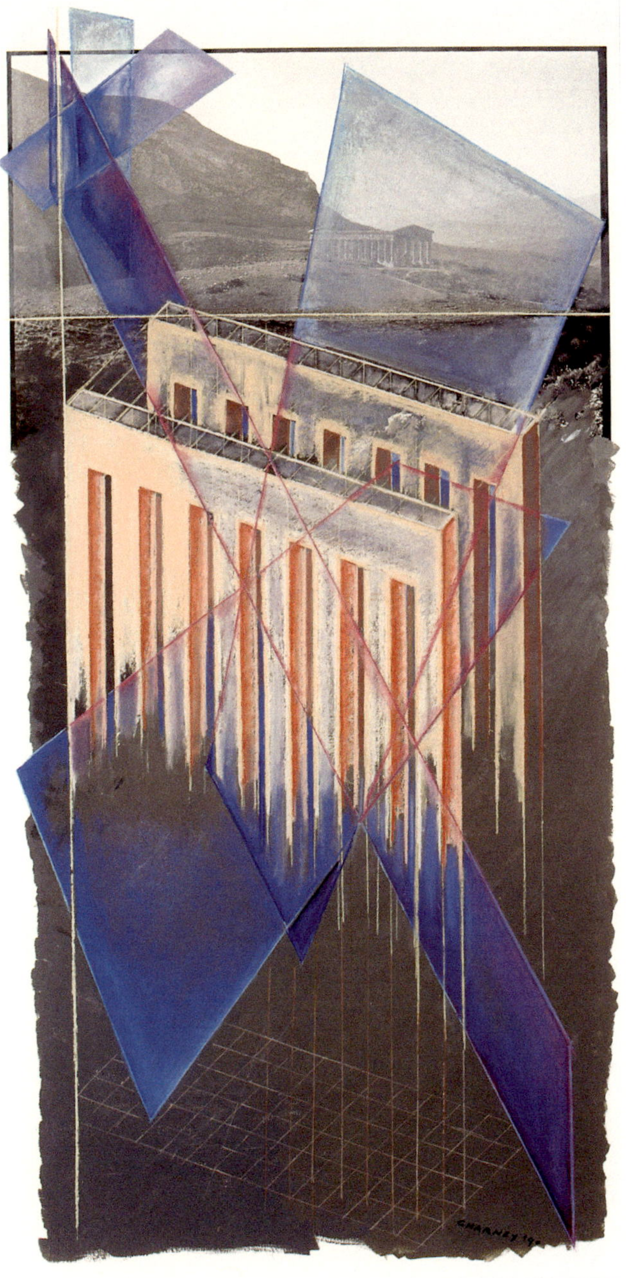

6   *Parable No. 4... Segesta* 1990

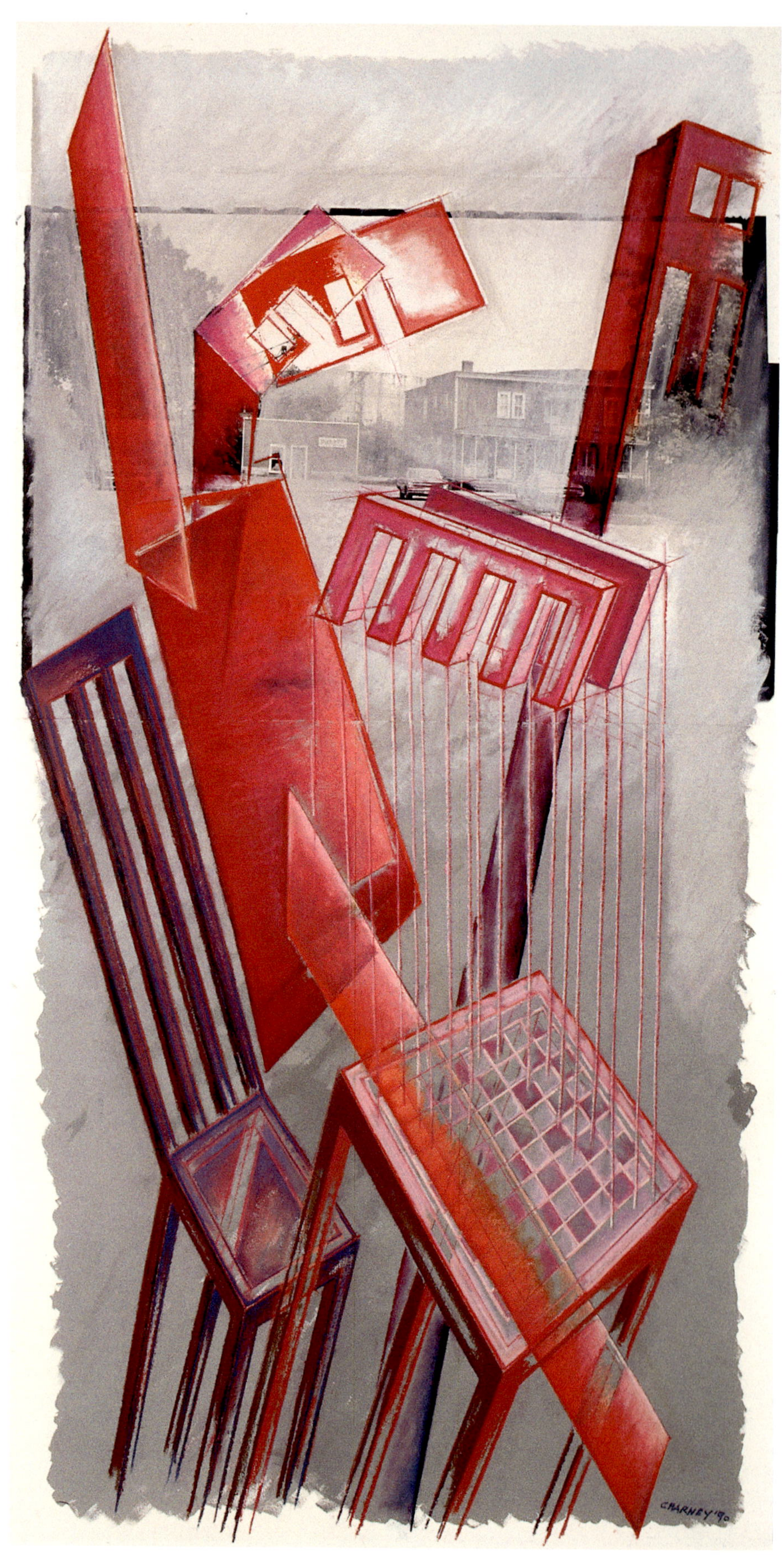

7   *Parable No. 5... Trois-Rivières* 1990

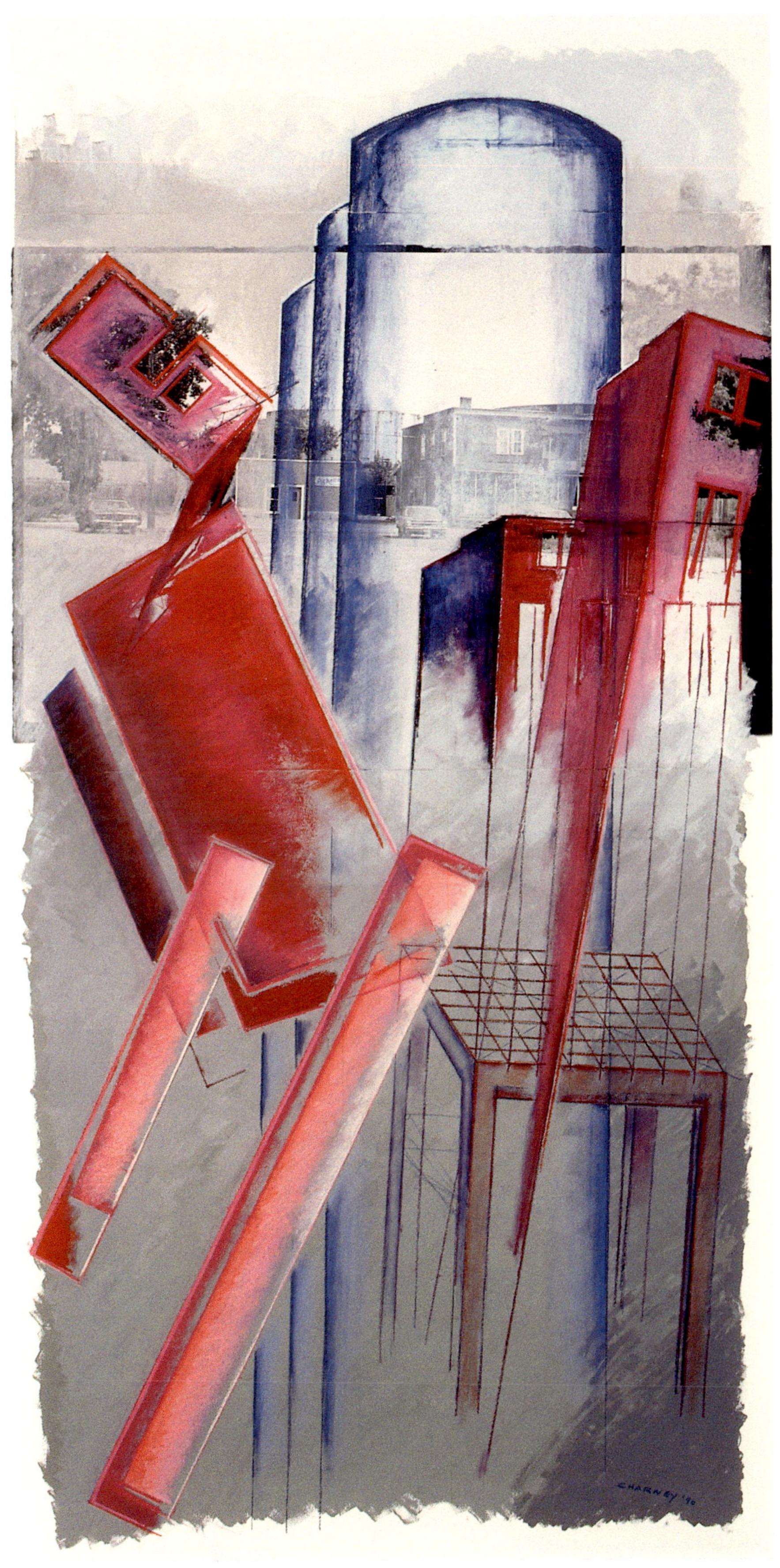

8   *Parable No. 6... Trois-Rivières* 1990

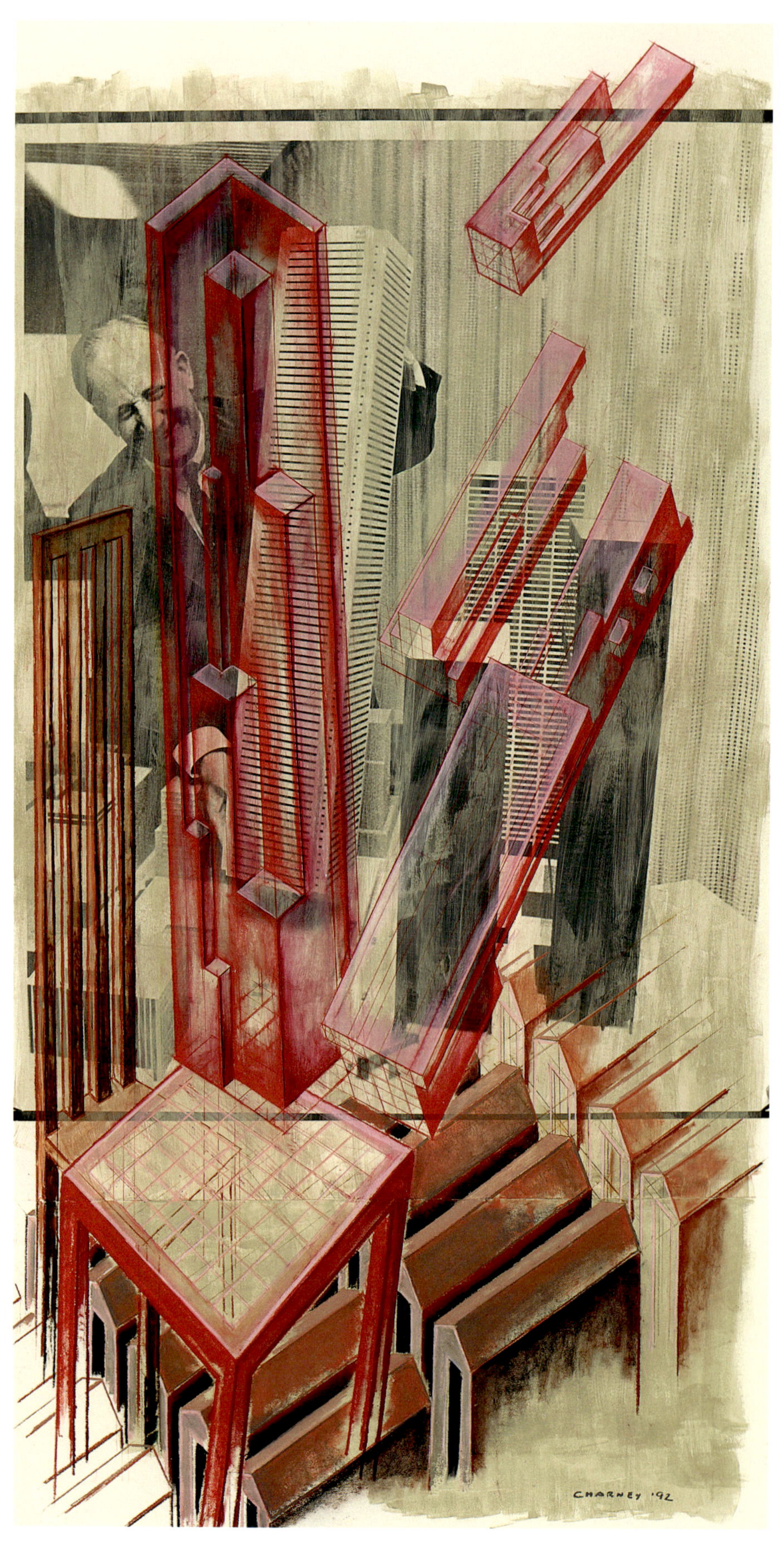

9   *Parable No. 11... so be it* 1992

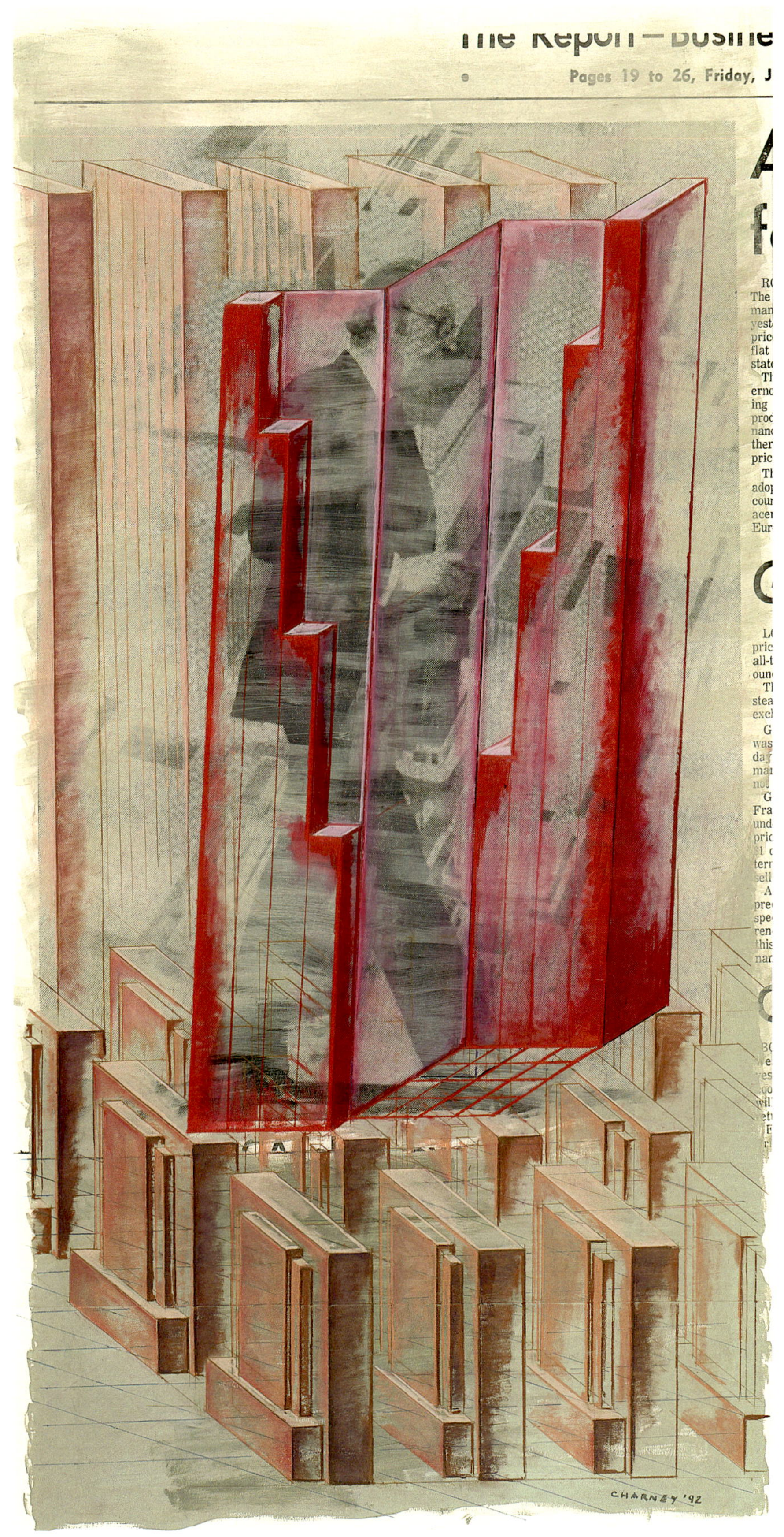

10   *Parable No. 12... RCA Corp. Expansion, New York* 1992

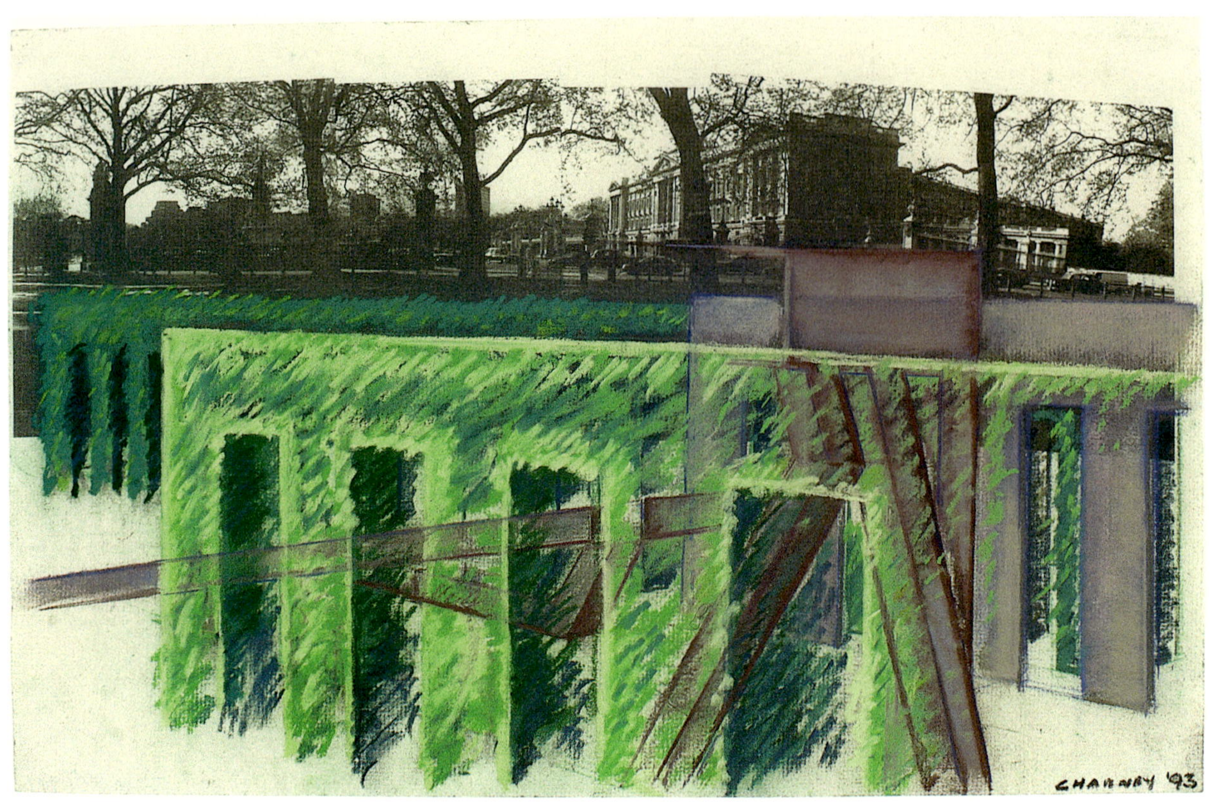

11   *CANADA MEMORIAL, Green Park, London... Study No. 7* 1993

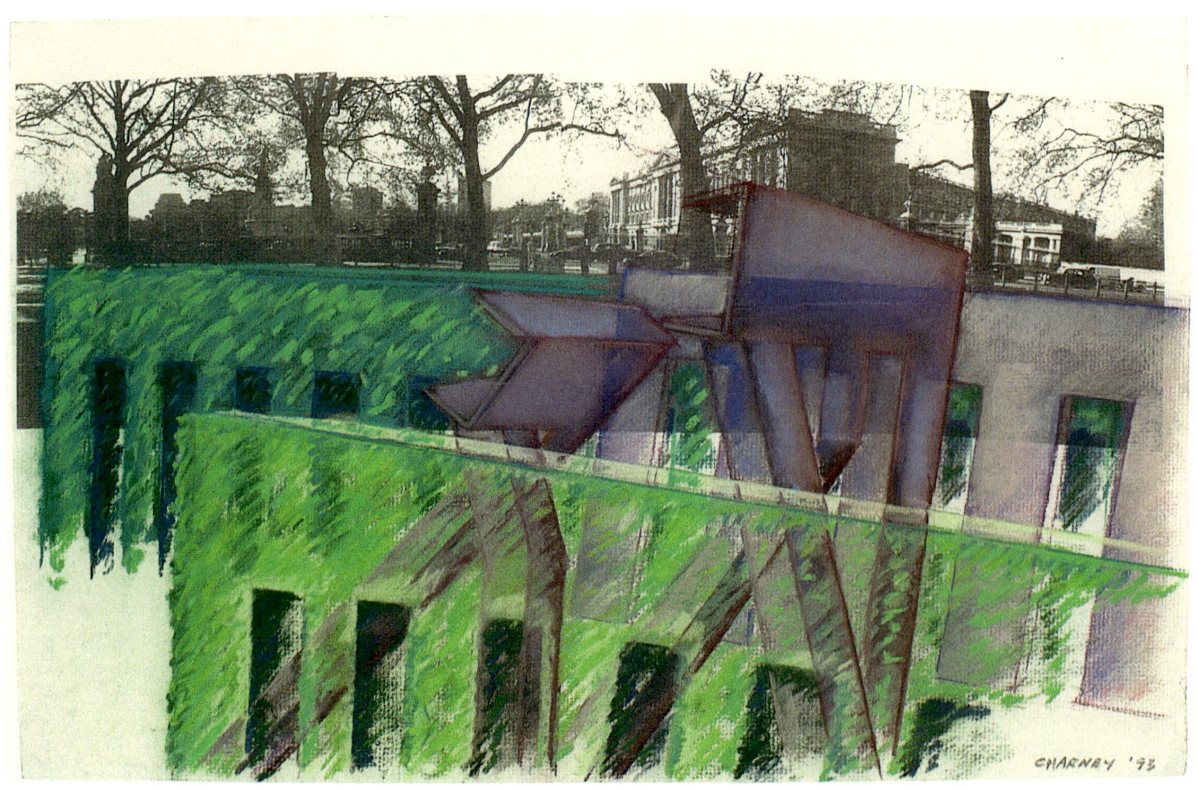

12   *CANADA MEMORIAL, Green Park, London... Study No. 8* 1993

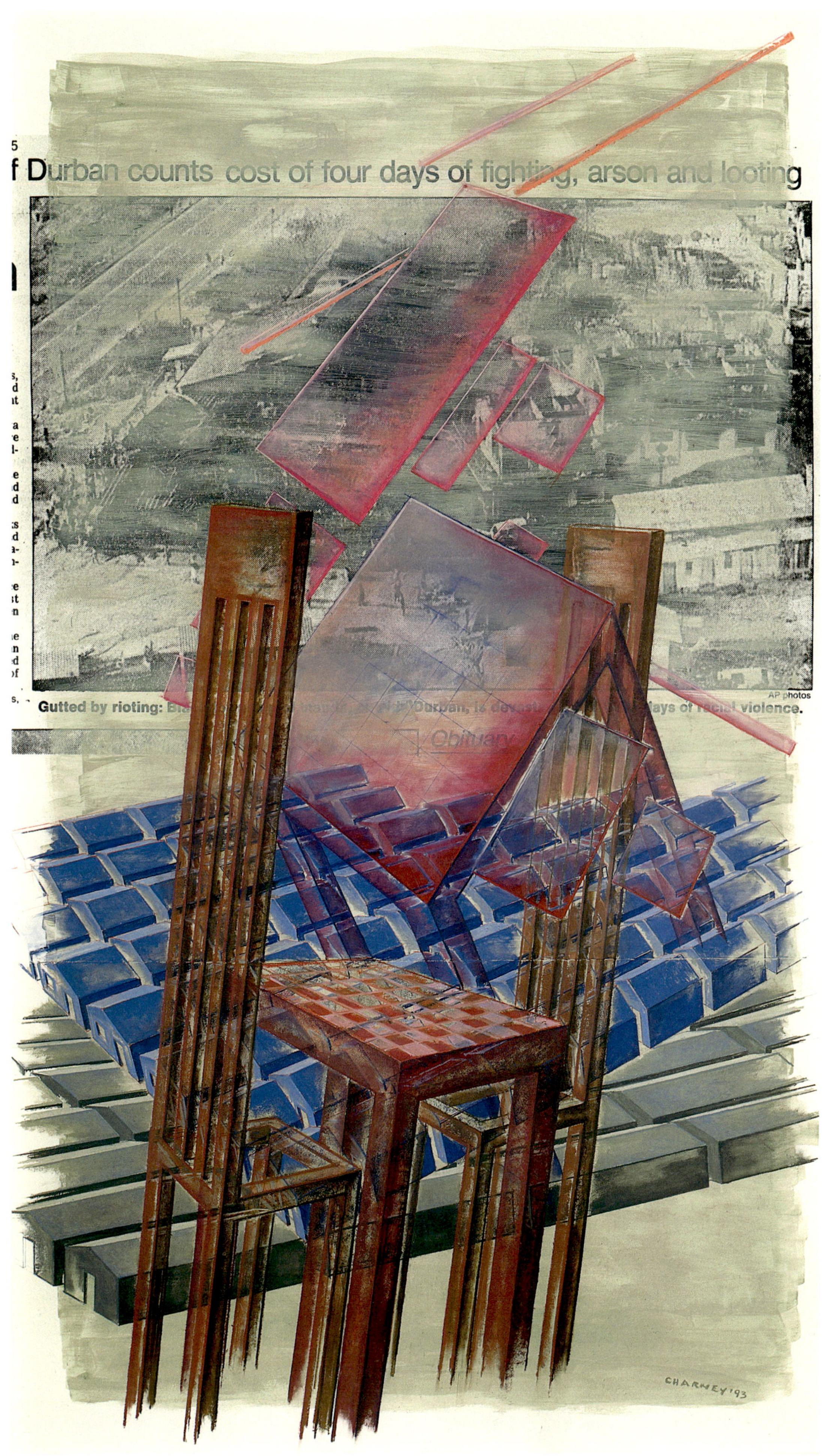

13   *After four days, Durban counts the cost...*   1993

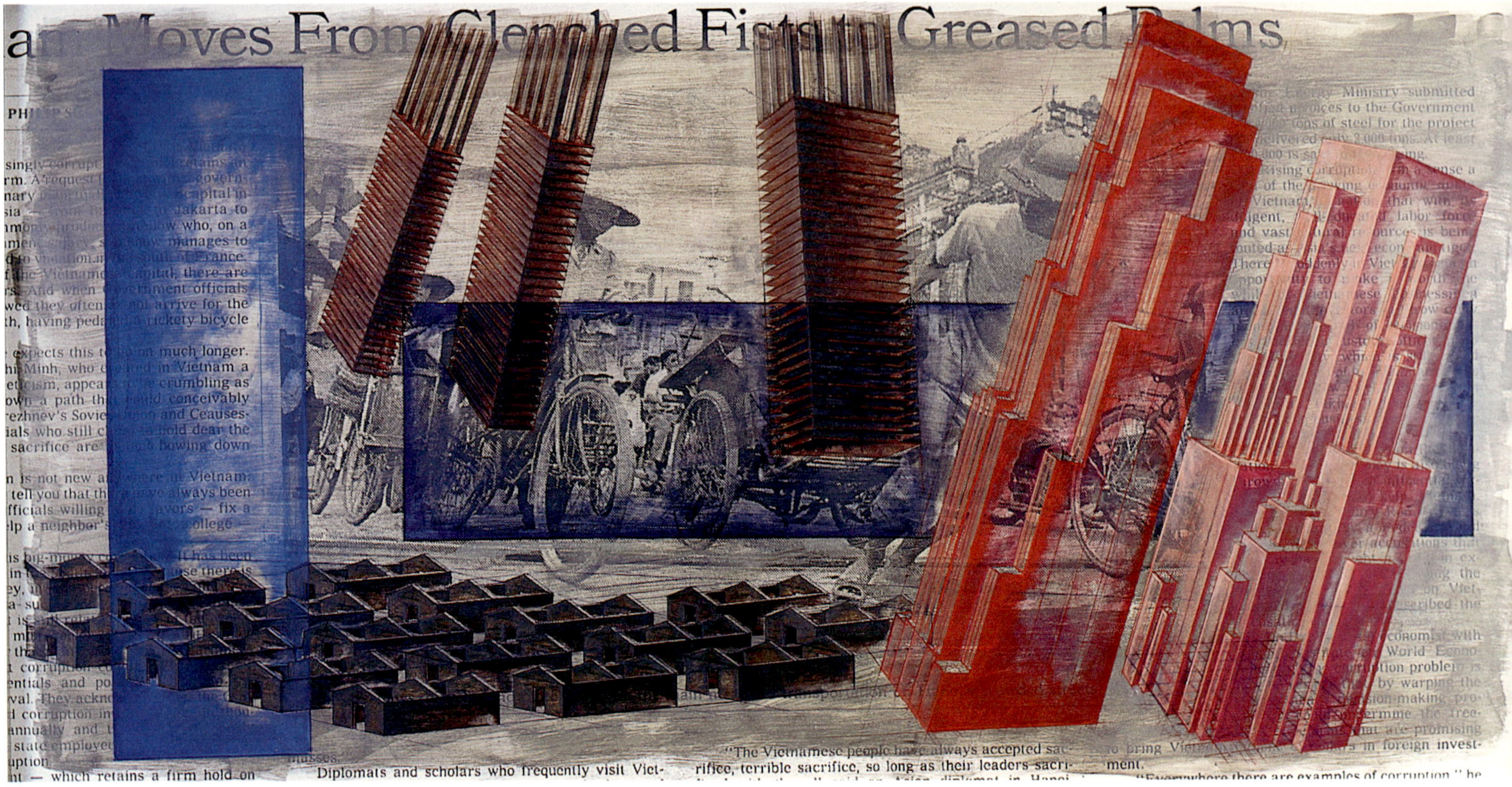

14   *PARABLE SERIES... Clenched Fists, Greased Palms* 1994

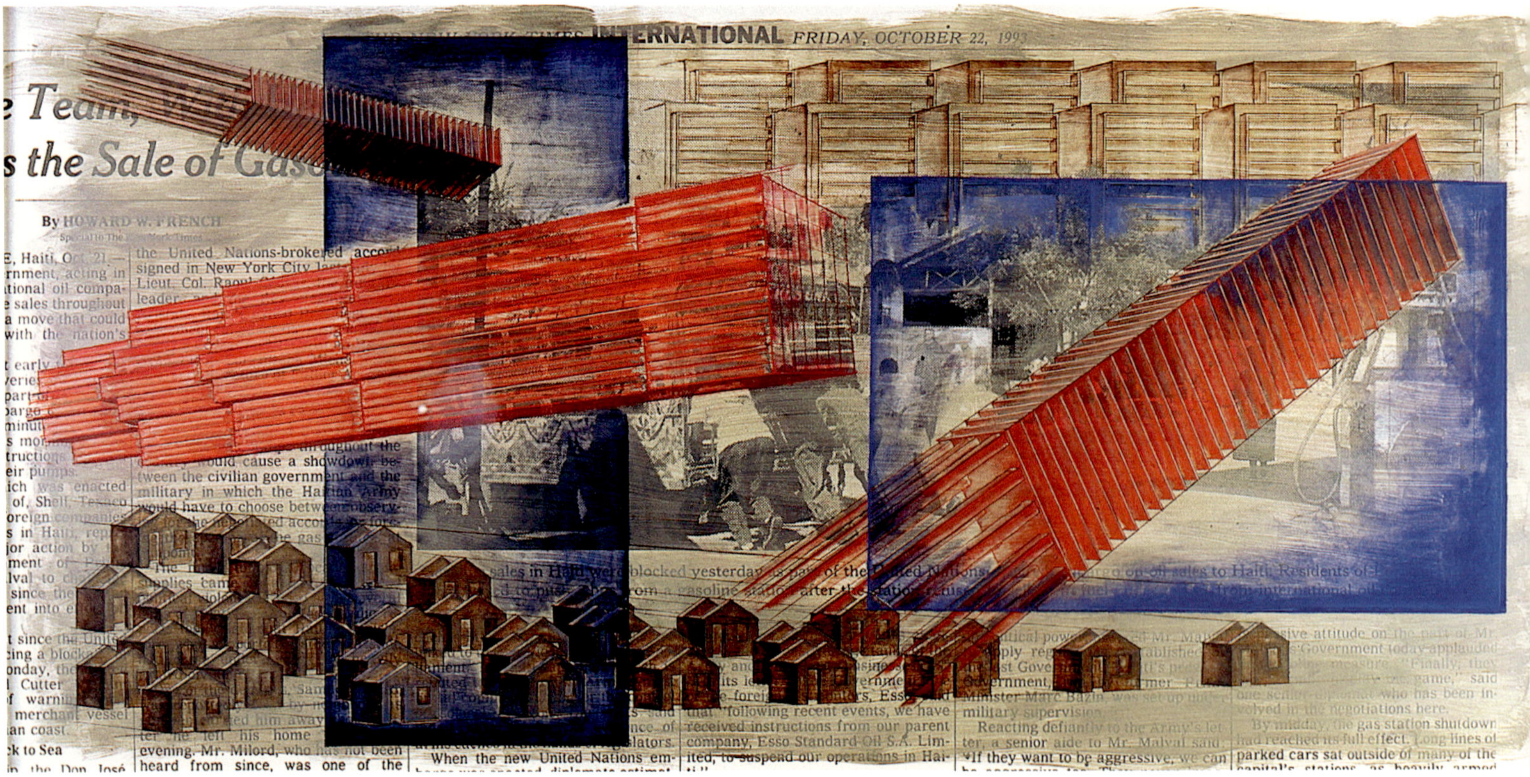

15   *PARABLE SERIES... With Help, Gasoline* 1994

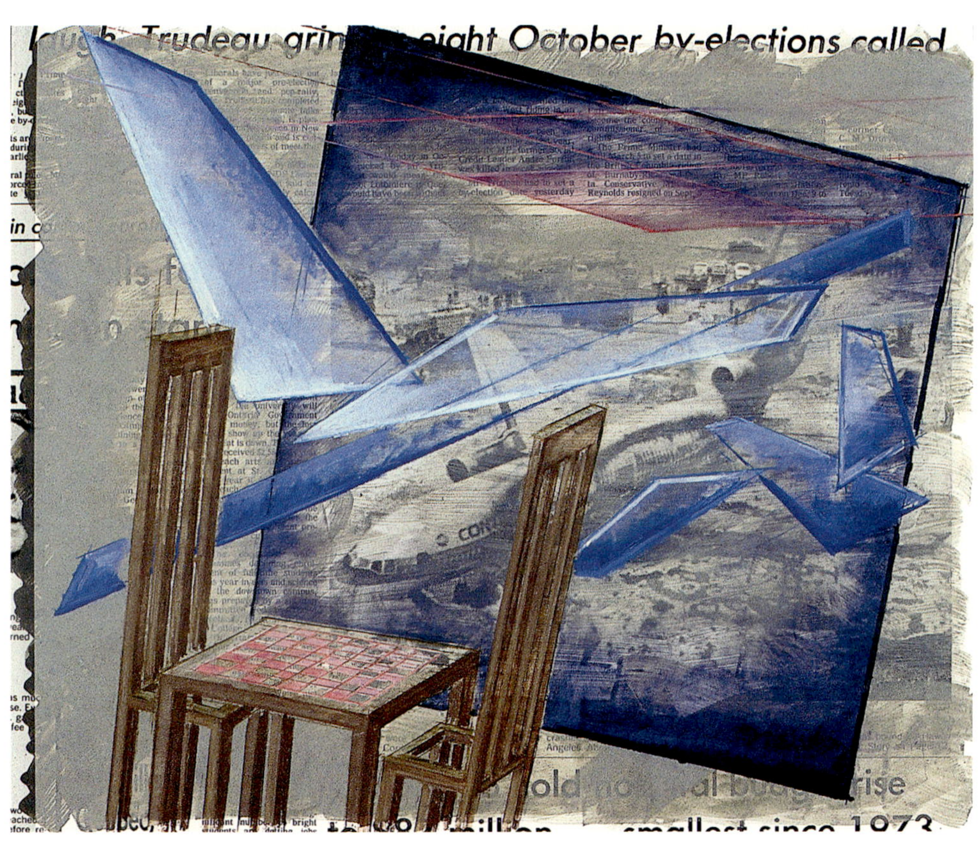

16   *IN FLIGHT SERIES... Continental Air, Los Angeles, 1978* 1994

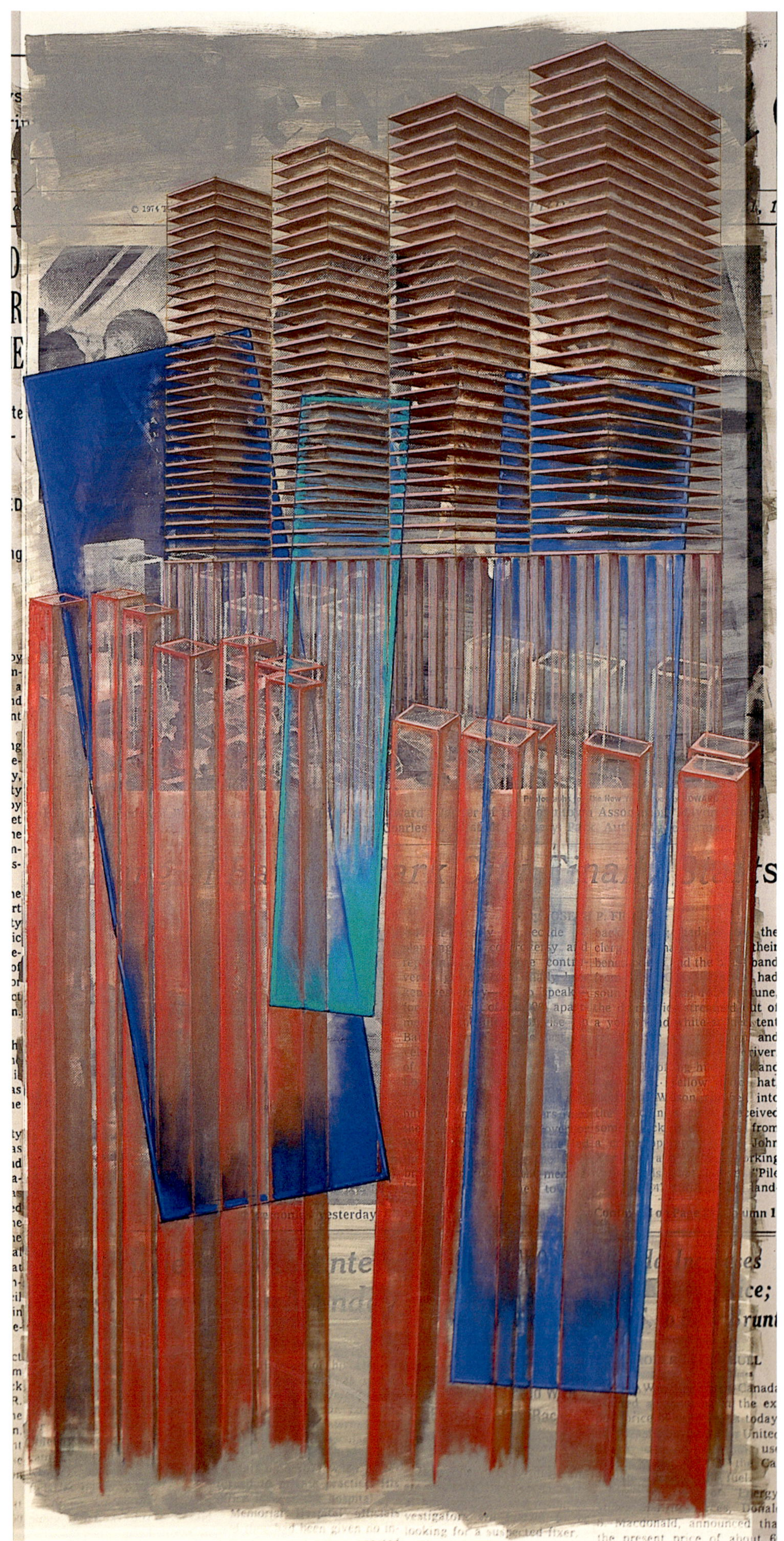

17   *Parable No. 22… Battery Park City Finally Starts, New York, 1974*   1994–95

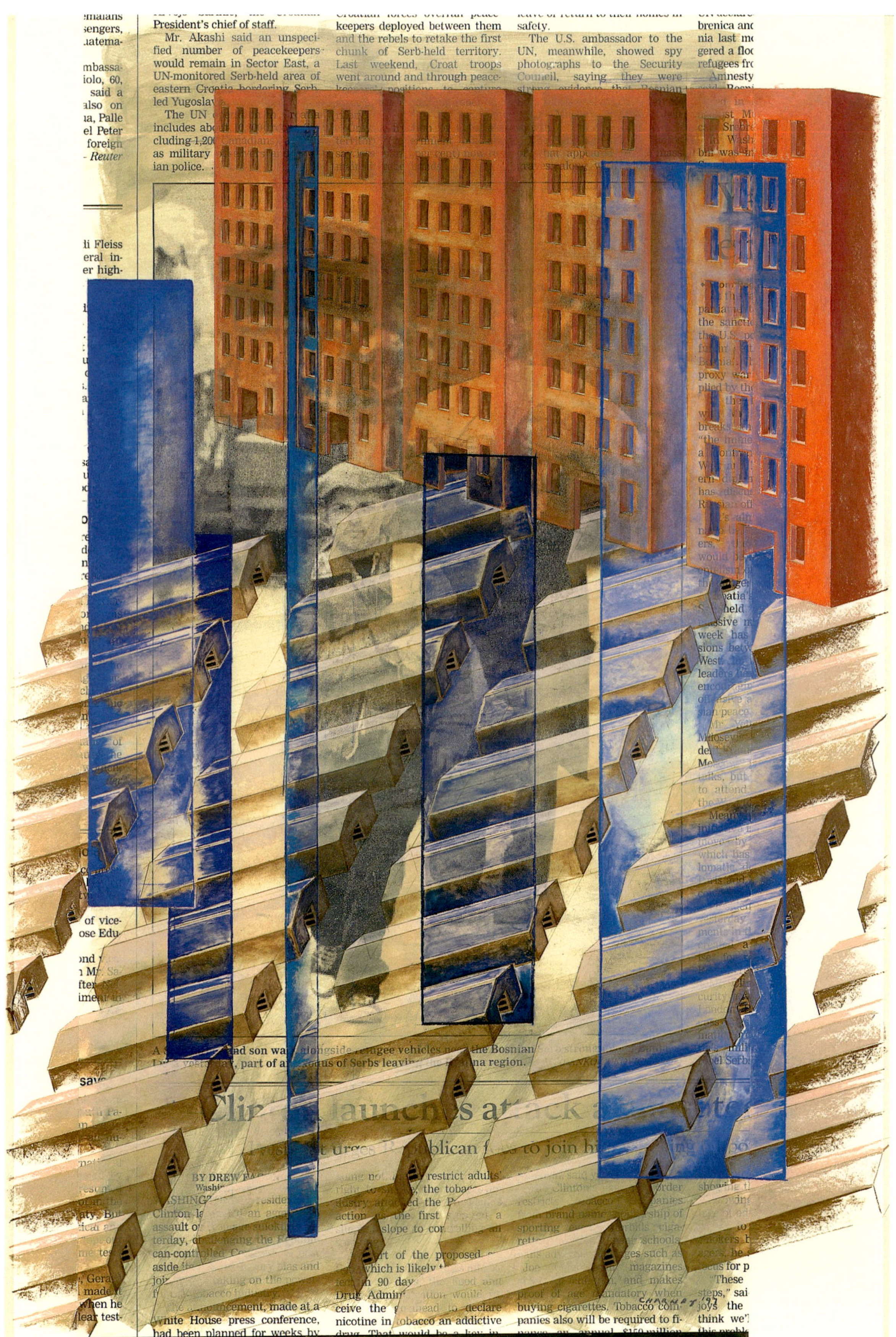

18   *Father and sons...* 1996–97

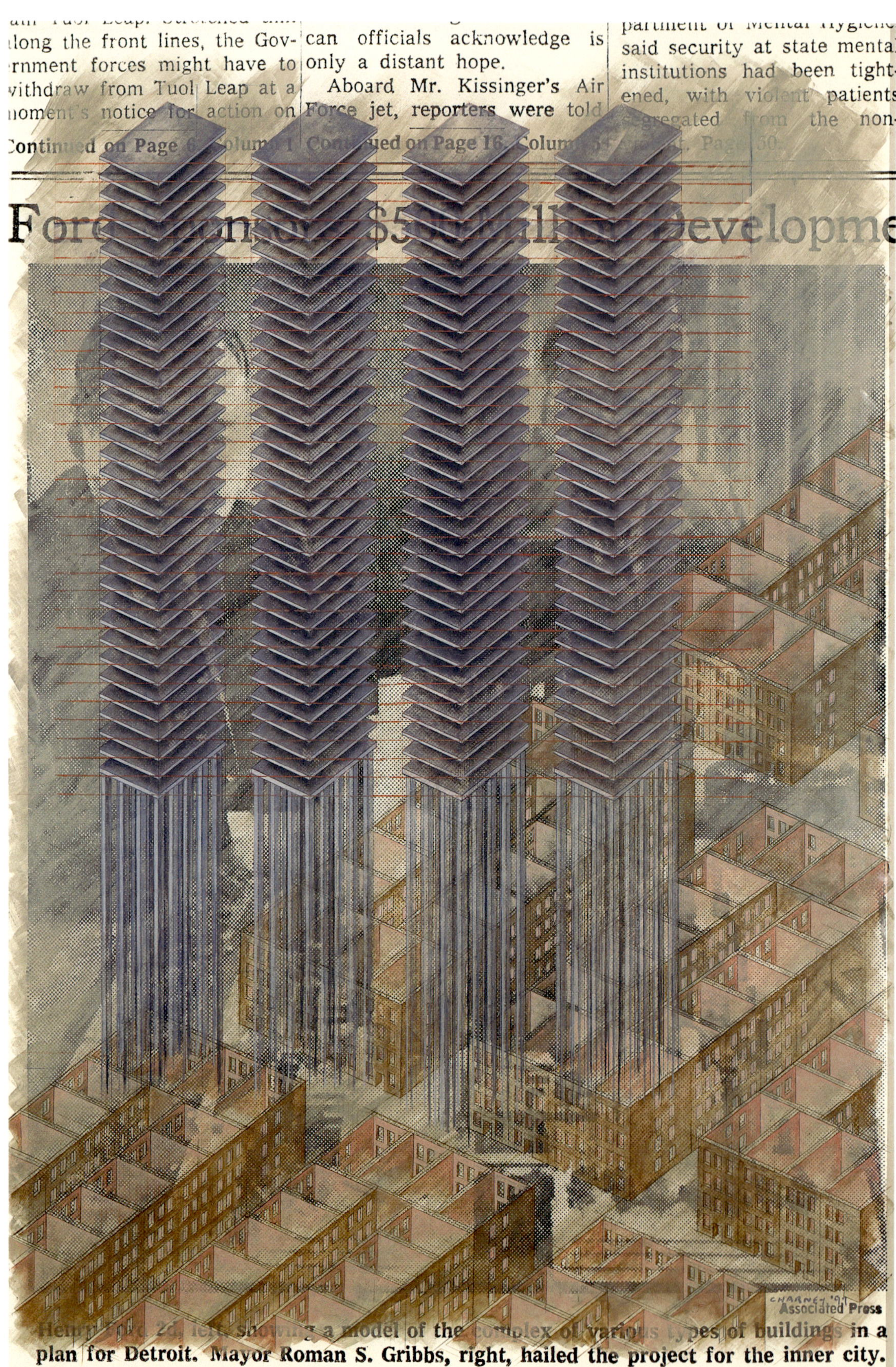

19   *THE AMERICAN CITY: Henry and Friends, Detroit, circa 1970… 1996–97*

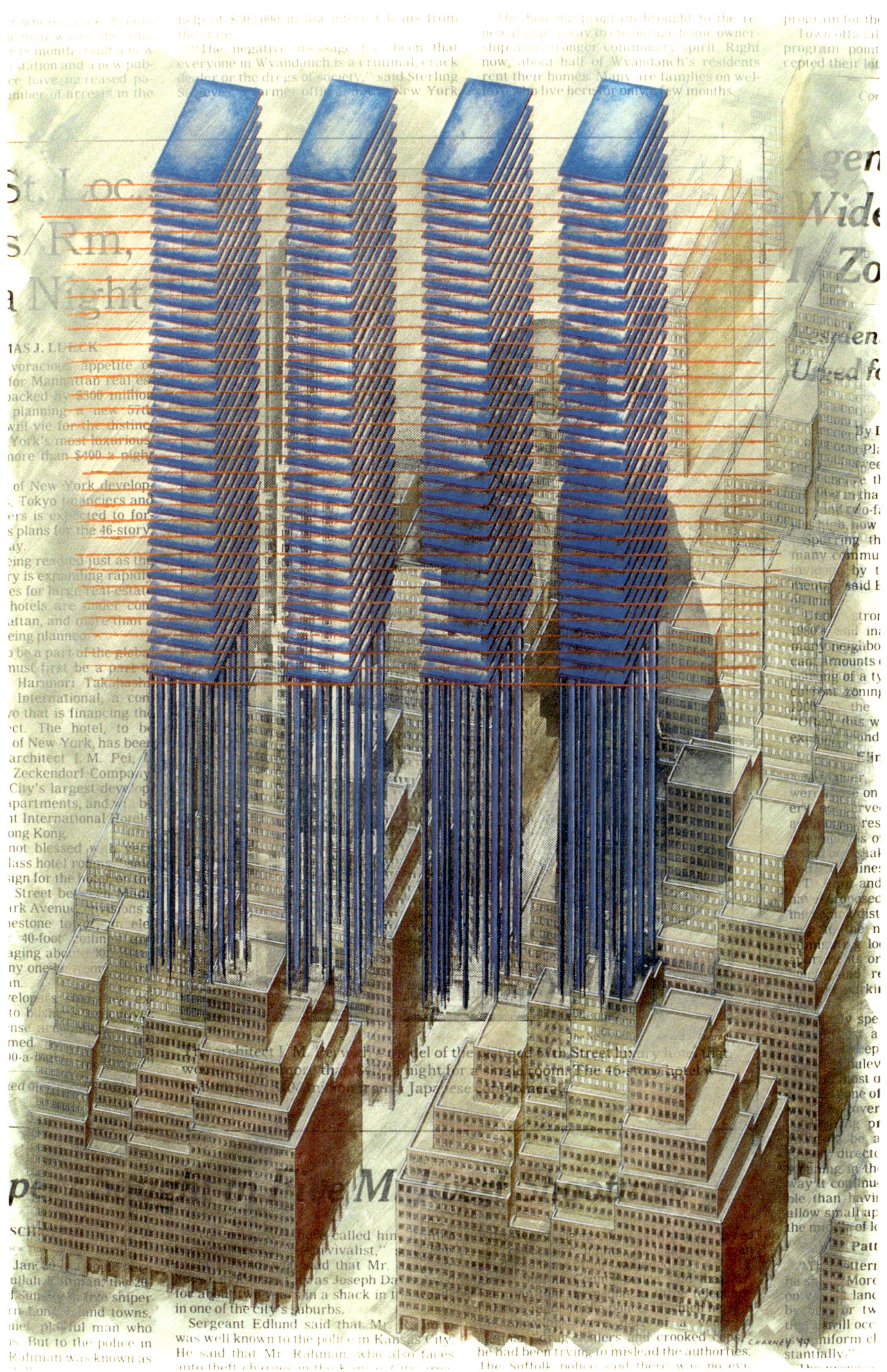

20   *THE AMERICAN CITY: Ieho Ming & Friends, Manhattan 1989* 1999–2000

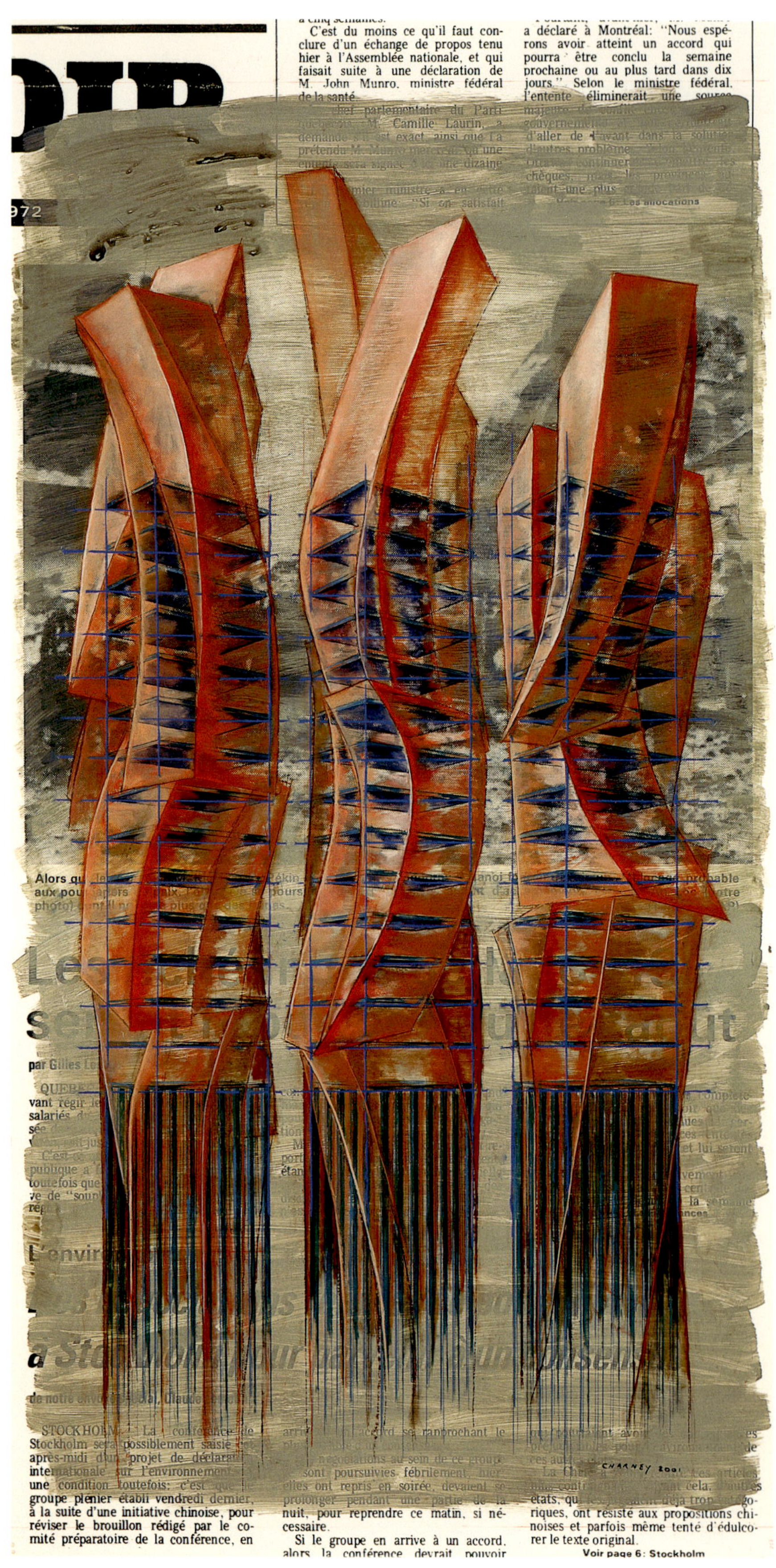

21   *THE AMERICAN CITY: via Saigon* 1999–2001

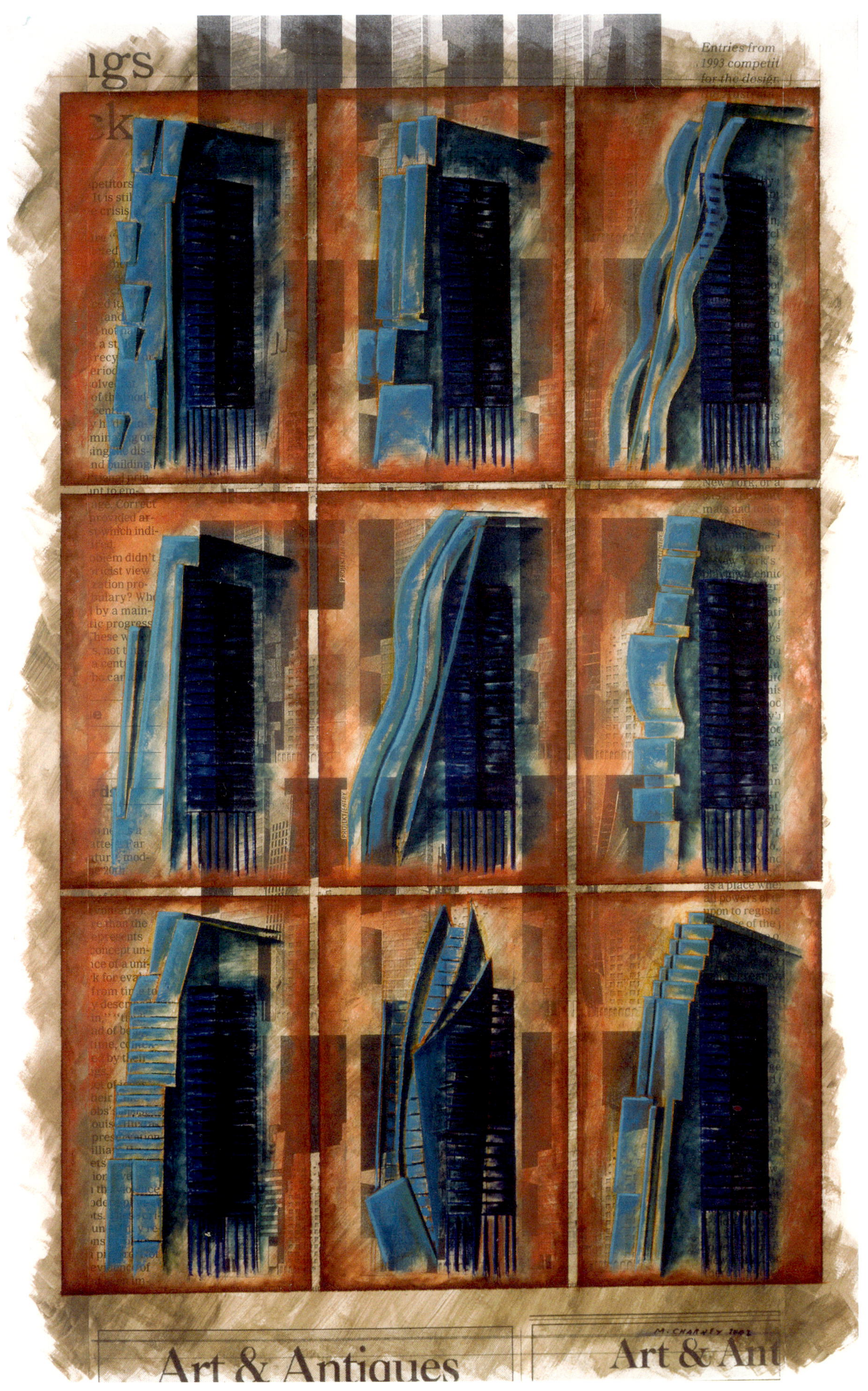
Art & Antiques
Art & Ant

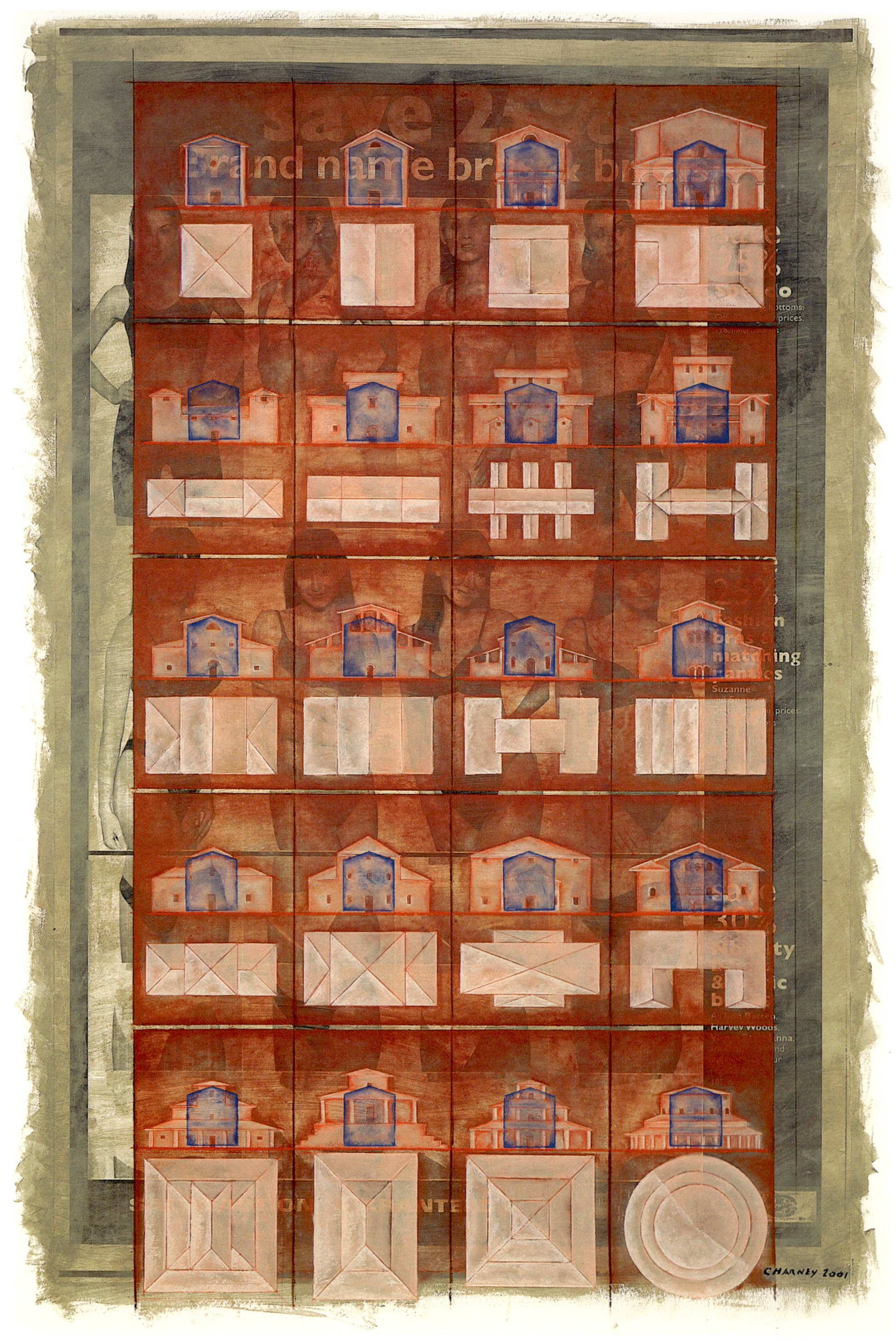

23   ONE FIT SIZES ALL/1: *Précis des Leçons d'Architecture, 1819, Combinaisons de Combles* 1999–2001

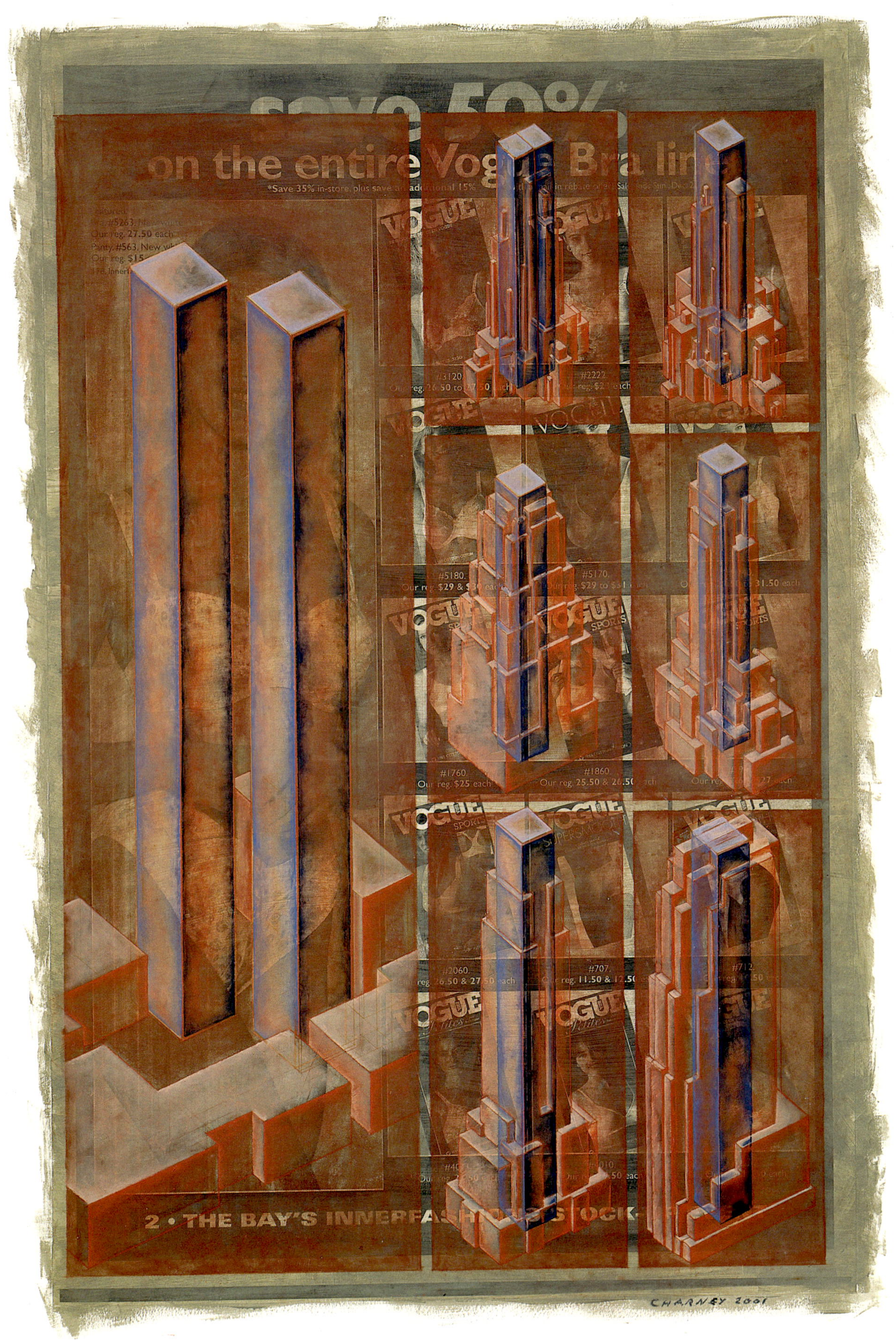

24   *ONE FIT SIZES ALL/2: 20th Century New York Skyscrapers* 1999–2001

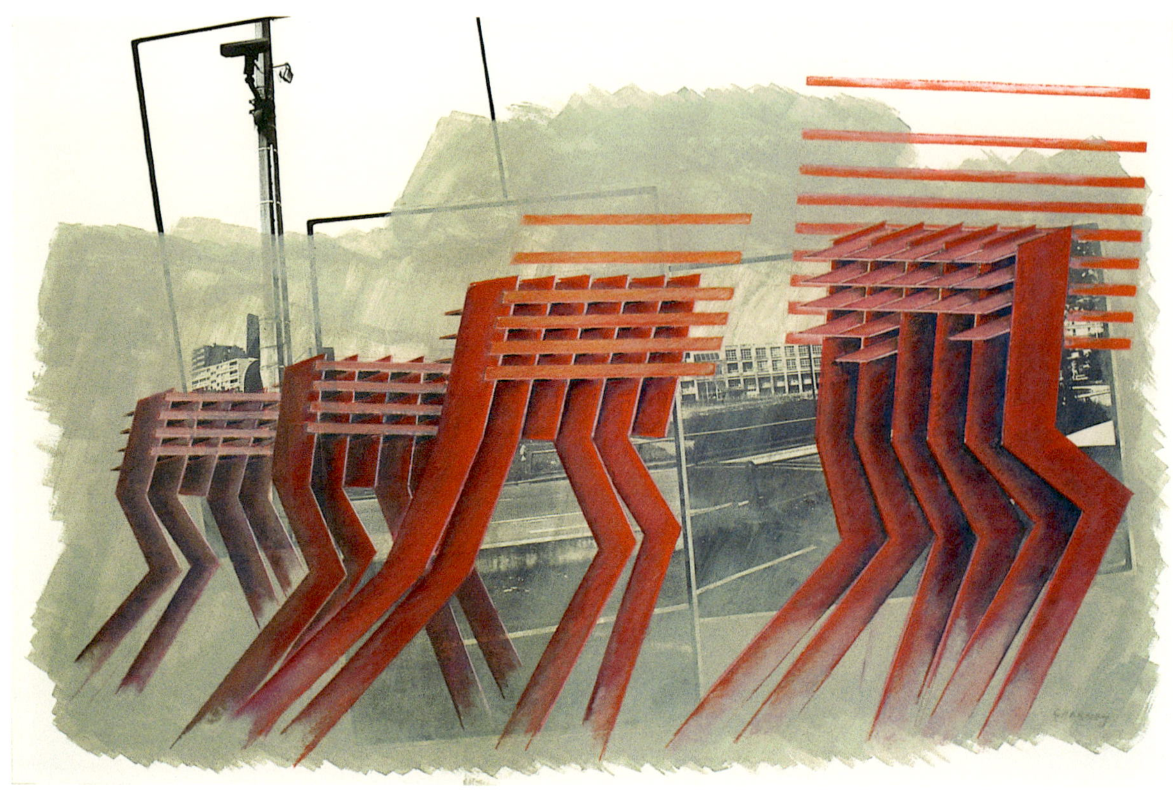

25   *CITIES ON THE RUN... Blocks in Search of a City*   1997–98

26   *CITIES ON THE RUN... Blocks Running Scared*   1997–98

27   *CITIES ON THE RUN... on the edges of industrial belts*   2002–05

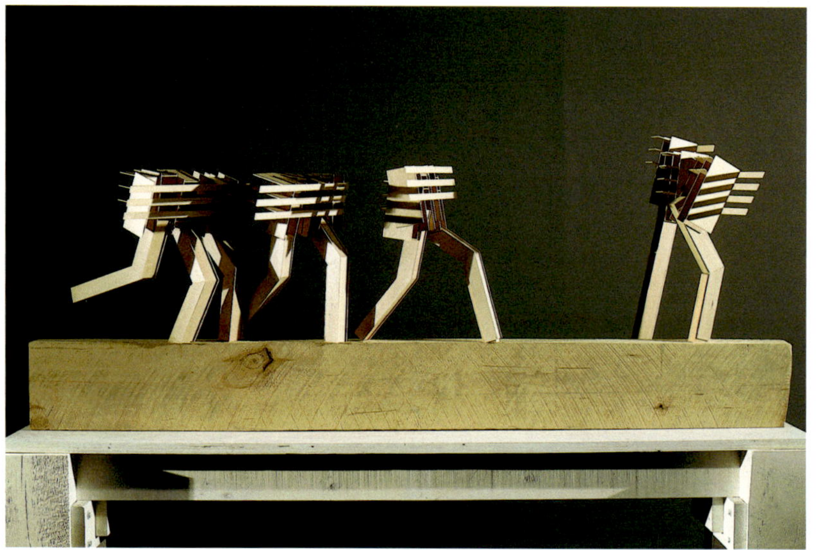

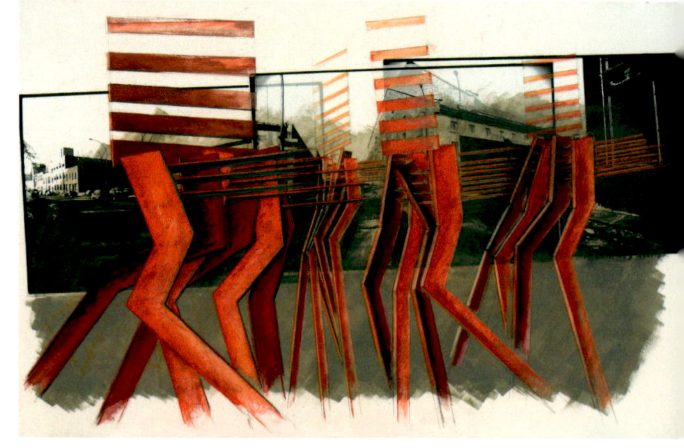

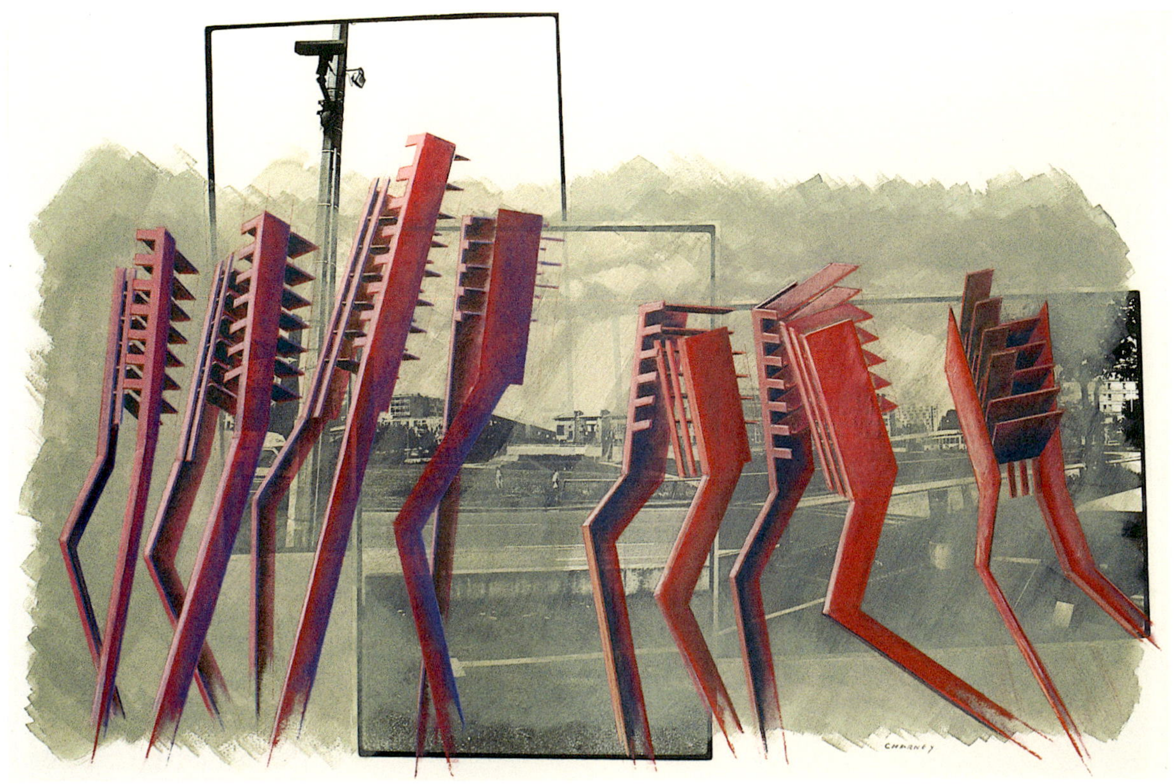

28   *CITIES ON THE RUN... Tenements in Search of Streets*   1996–98

29   *CITIES ON THE RUN... Tenements on the Move*   1996–98

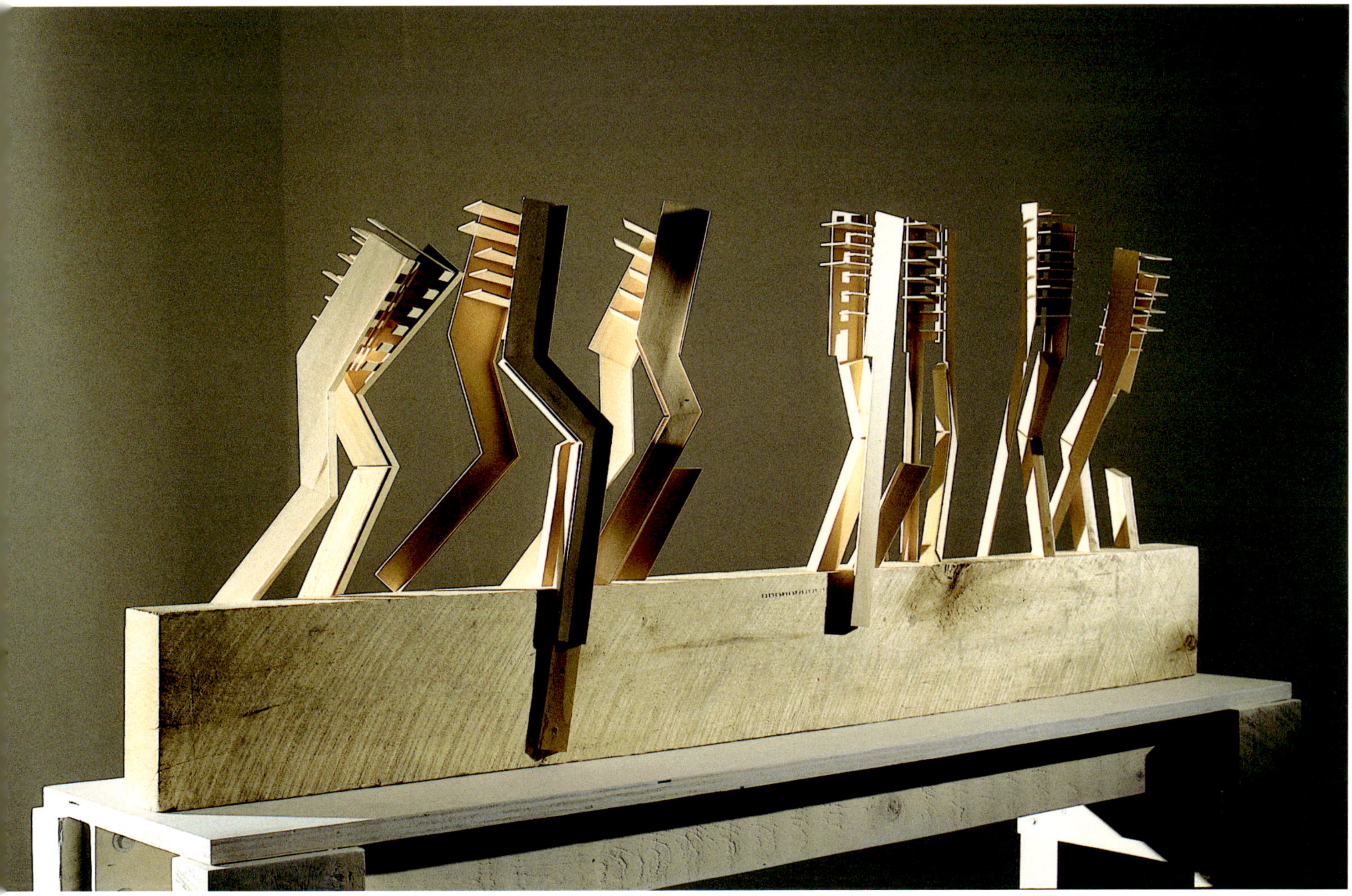

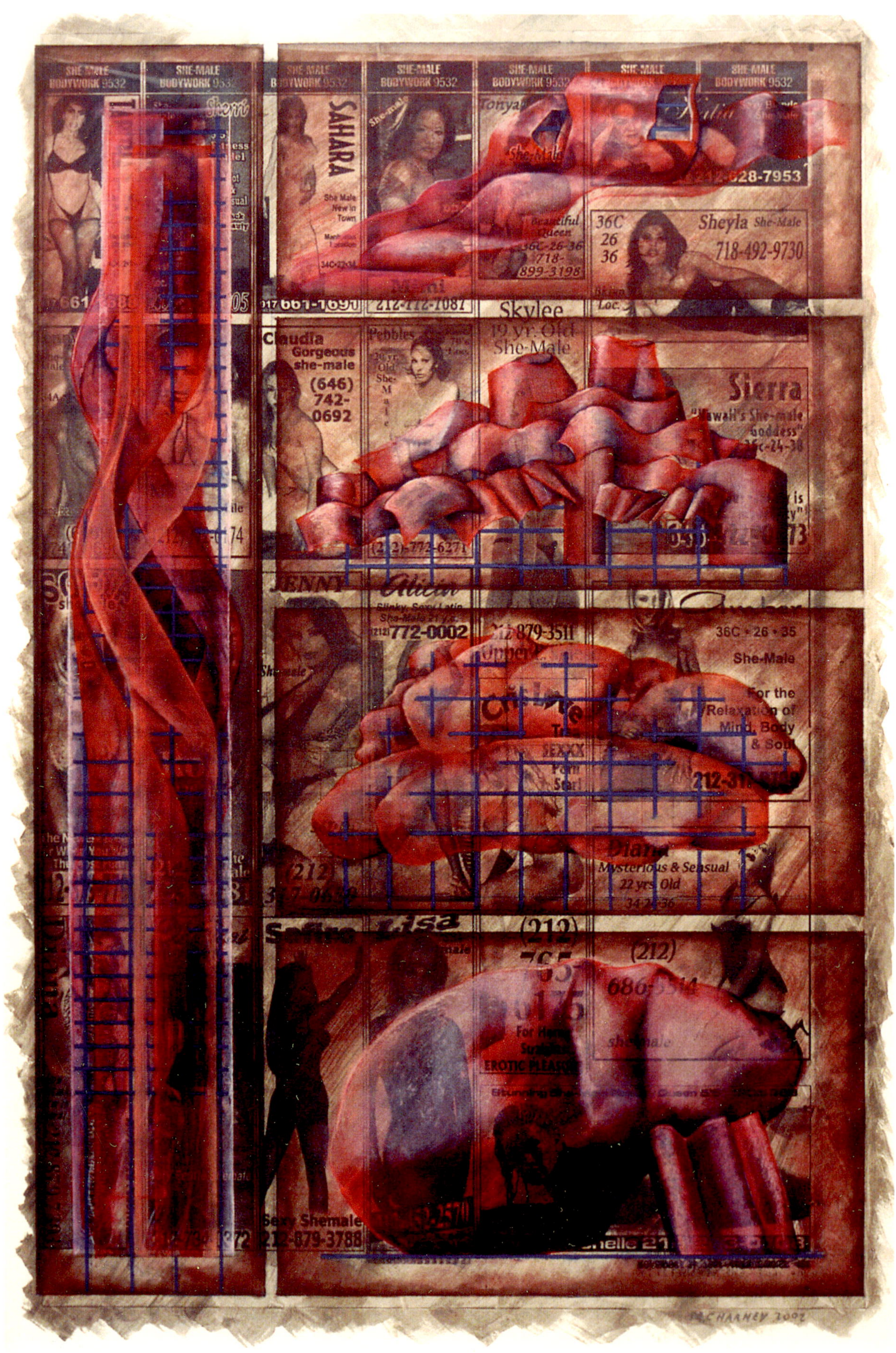

30   *ONE FIT SIZES ALL/3: Blobs on the Grid...*   2002

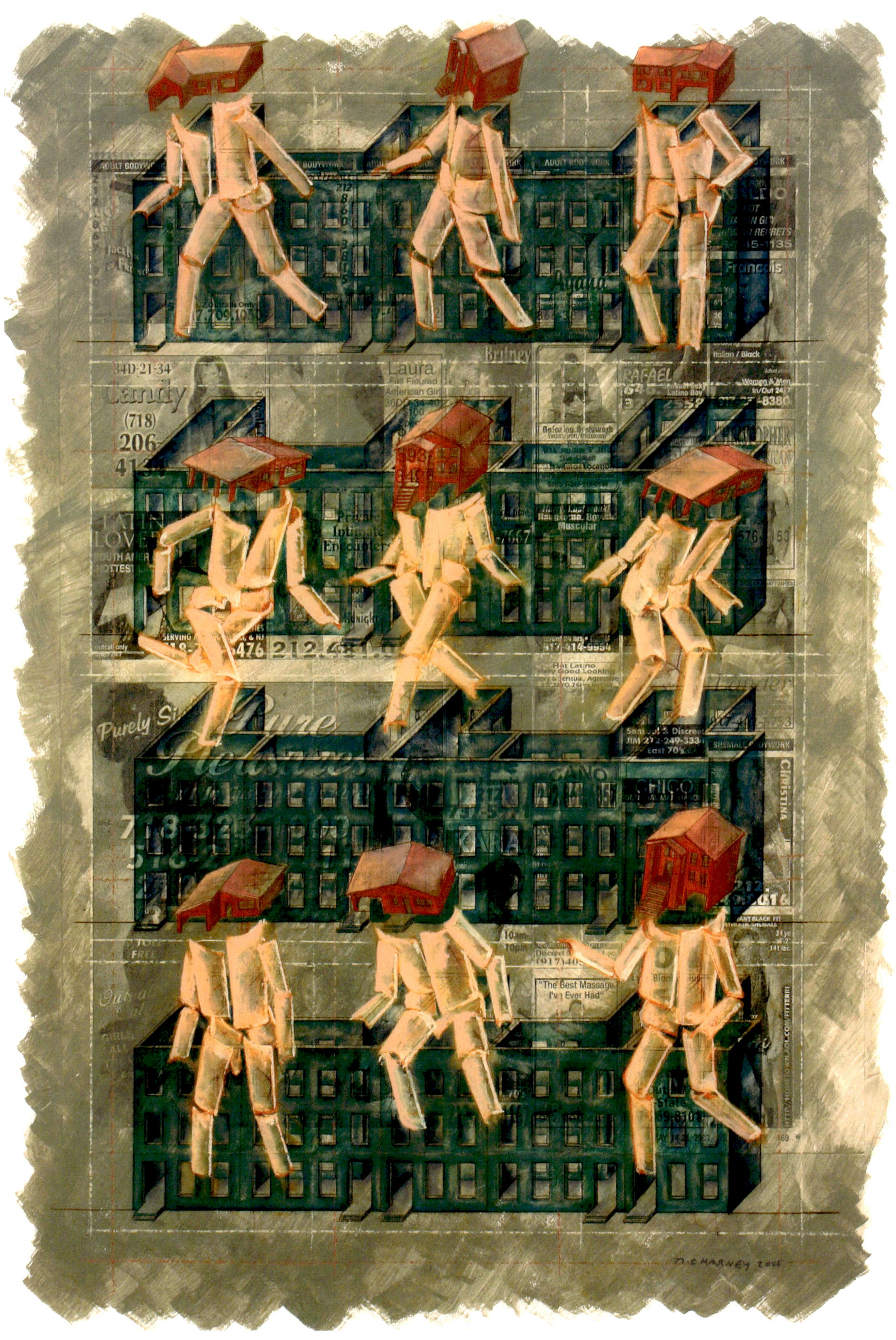

31   *CITIES ON THE MOVE... the swinging burbs*   2003–06

Exhibition Checklist

1. *THE SITE... Les Maisons de la rue*
   1976
   Gelatin silver print.
   36.1 x 49.1 cm (16 x 20 in.)
   Canadian Centre for Architecture, Montréal

2. *THE SITE ALTERED... Les Maisons de la rue*
   1976
   Gelatin silver print of a photomontage on fiber paper
   36.2 x 50.4 cm (16 x 20 in.)
   Canadian Centre for Architecture, Montréal

3. *Les Maisons de la rue Sherbrooke*
   1976
   Film by Roger Cantin
   Production: Marc Daigle, ACPAV, Montréal

4. *In Flight... de Stijl as a Prairie Dog*
   1990
   Oil pastel and acrylic on a gelatin silver print and
   wove paper, mounted on Masonite
   188 x 91.5 cm (74 x 36 in.)
   Richard Cooper Collection, Toronto

5. *Parable No. 3... La Prairie*
   1990
   Oil pastel, acrylic, and colored pencil on a gelatin
   silver print and wove paper, mounted on Masonite
   188 x 91.5 cm (74 x 36 in.)
   National Gallery of Canada, Ottawa
   Gift of Martin Storm, Toronto, 1998

6. *Parable No. 4... Segesta*
   1990
   Oil pastel, acrylic, and colored pencil on a gelatin
   silver print and wove paper, mounted on Masonite
   188 x 91.5 cm (74 x 36 in.)
   National Gallery of Canada, Ottawa
   Gift of Martin Storm, Toronto, 1998

7. *Parable No. 5... Trois-Rivières*
   1990
   Oil pastel and acrylic on a gelatin silver print and wove
   paper, mounted on Masonite
   244 x 122 cm (96⅛ x 48 in.)
   Musée des beaux-arts de Montréal

8. *Parable No. 6... Trois-Rivières*
   1990
   Oil pastel and acrylic on a gelatin silver print and wove
   paper, mounted on Masonite
   244 x 122 cm (96⅛ x 48 in.)
   Musée des beaux-arts de Montréal

9. *Parable No. 11... so be it*
   1992
   Oil pastel and acrylic on a gelatin silver print, mounted
   on museum board
   244 x 122 cm (96⅛ x 48 in.)
   National Gallery of Canada, Ottawa
   Gift of Martin E. Kovnats, Toronto, 1998

10. *Parable No. 12... RCA Corp. Expansion, New York*
    1992
    Oil pastel and acrylic on a gelatin silver print, mounted
    on board
    243.8 x 121.8 cm (96⅛ x 48 in.)
    Jared Sable Collection, Toronto

11. *CANADA MEMORIAL, Green Park, London... Study No. 7*
    1993
    Pastel on a laser print of a photomontage (Green Park,
    Buckingham Palace, 1992) on paper
    45.3 x 61 cm (17¾ x 24 in.)
    Jared Sable Collection, Toronto

12. *CANADA MEMORIAL, Green Park, London... Study No. 8*
    1993
    Pastel on a laser print of a photomontage (Green Park,
    Buckingham Palace, 1992) on paper
    45.3 x 61 cm (17¾ x 24 in.)
    Jared Sable Collection, Toronto

13. *After four days, Durban counts the cost...*
    1993
    Oil pastel and acrylic on a gelatin silver print, mounted
    on museum board
    213.4 x 122 cm (84 x 48 in.)
    Musée des beaux-arts de Montréal
    Gift of Dr. & Mrs. Richard Rodney and family

14. *PARABLE SERIES... Clenched Fists, Greased Palms*
    1994
    Oil pastel and acrylic on a gelatin silver print on fiber
    paper, mounted on board
    121.8 x 238.4 cm (48 x 93⅞ in.)
    Musée d'art contemporain de Montréal

15. *PARABLE SERIES... With Help, Gasoline*
    1994
    Oil pastel and acrylic on a gelatin silver print on fiber
    paper, mounted on board
    121.8 x 243.8 cm. (48 x 96 in.)
    Amesbury Chalmers Collection, Toronto

16. *IN FLIGHT SERIES... Continental Air, Los Angeles,
    1978*
    1994
    Oil pastel and acrylic on a gelatin silver print on fiber
    paper, mounted on board
    55 x 66 cm (21.7 x 26 in.)
    Ruth and Sam Karpman Collection, Montréal

17. *Parable No. 22... Battery Park City Finally Starts,
    New York, 1974*
    1994–95
    Oil pastel and acrylic on a gelatin silver print, mounted
    on board
    243.8 x 121.8 cm (96 x 48 in.)
    Caisse de Dépôt du Québec Collection, New York Office

18. *Father and sons...*
    1996–97
    Oil pastel and acrylic on a laser print on paper, mounted
    on board
    182.5 x 121.7 cm. (71⅞ x 47⅞ in.)
    Norman Damiani and Hélène Barabé Collection,
    Montréal

19. *THE AMERICAN CITY: Henry and Friends, Detroit,
    circa 1970...*
    1996–97
    Oil pastel and acrylic on a gelatin silver print, mounted
    on board
    186 x 121.5 cm (73¼ x 47¾ in.)
    Musée national des beaux-arts du Québec

20. *THE AMERICAN CITY: Ieho Ming & Friends,
    Manhattan 1989*
    1999–2000
    Oil pastel and acrylic on a gelatin silver print, mounted
    on archival board
    188.5 x 121.5 cm. (74¼ x 47⅞ in.)
    Musée national des beaux-arts du Québec
    Gift of Dara A. Charney

21. *THE AMERICAN CITY: via Saigon*
    1999–2001
    Oil pastel and acrylic on a gelatin silver print, mounted
    on archival board
    228.5 x 122 cm. (90 x 48 in.)
    Norman Damiani and Hélène Barabé Collection,
    Montréal

22. *ONE FIT SIZES ALL/4: From J.L. Durand to Manhattan
    Skyscraper Culture*
    2002
    Oil pastel and acrylic on a laser print, mounted on
    archival board
    182.4 x 111.7 cm. (71⅞ x 44 in.)
    Bella and Irving Borwick Collection, New York

23. *ONE FIT SIZES ALL/1: Précis des Leçons
    d'Architecture, 1819, Combinaisons de Combles*
    1999–2001
    Oil pastel and acrylic on a laser print mounted on
    museum quality board
    152.4 x 101.8 cm. (60 x 40 in.)
    Gordon Ridgley Collection, Toronto

24. *ONE FIT SIZES ALL/2: 20th Century New York
    Skyscrapers*
    1999–2001
    Oil pastel and acrylic on a laser print, mounted on
    museum quality board
    152.4 x 101.8 cm. (60 x 40 in.)
    Norman Damiani and Hélène Barabé Collection,
    Montréal

25. *CITIES ON THE RUN... Blocks in Search of a City*
    1997–98
    Acrylic and oil pastel on a montage of three laser prints
    of original photographs on 100% cotton rag, 20 lb.
    vellum, mounted on board
    101.5 x 152 cm. (40 x 59¾ in.)
    Private Collection, Montréal

26. *CITIES ON THE RUN... Blocks Running Scared*
    1997–98
    Wood, partly lacquered
    160 x 172.5 x 42 cm. (63 x 67⅞ x 16½ in.)
    Collection of the artist

27. *CITIES ON THE RUN... on the edges of industrial belts*
    2002–05
    Oil pastel and acrylic on a montage of three laser prints
    of original photographs, mounted on board
    101.5 x 152.5 cm. (40 x 60 in.)
    Rosamond Ivey Collection, Toronto

28. *CITIES ON THE RUN... Tenements in Search of Streets*
    1996–98
    Acrylic and oil pastel on a montage of three laser prints
    of original photographs on 100% cotton rag, 20 lb.
    vellum, mounted on board
    101.5 x 152 cm. (40 x 59⅞ in.)
    Private Collection, Montréal

29. *CITIES ON THE RUN... Tenements on the Move*
    1996–98
    Wood, partly lacquered
    163 x 170 x 40 cm. (64¼ x 66⅞ x 15¾ in.)
    Collection of the artist

30. *ONE FIT SIZES ALL/3: Blobs on the Grid...*
    2002
    Oil pastel and acrylic on a laser print, mounted on
    archival board
    182.4 x 111.7 cm. (71⅞ x 44 in.)
    Collection of the artist

31. *CITIES ON THE MOVE... the swinging burbs*
    2003–06
    Oil pastel and acrylic on a laser print, mounted on
    archival board
    152.5 x 101.5 cm. (60 x 40 in.)
    Collection of the artist

About the Artist

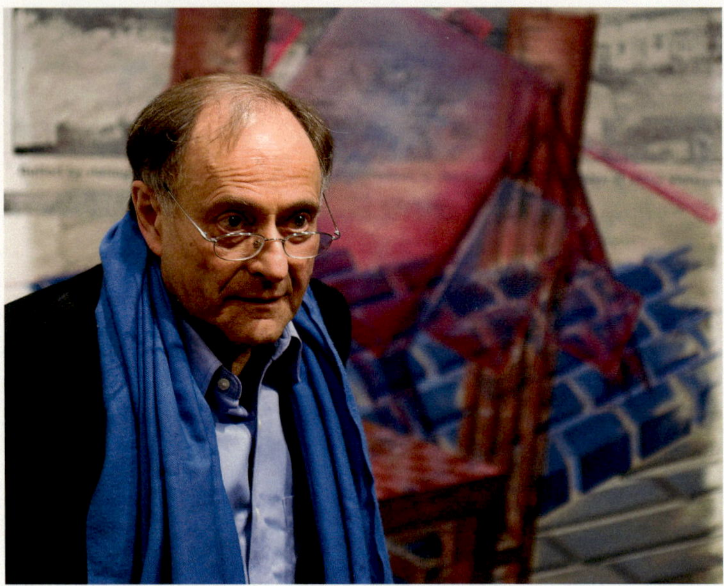

Melvin Charney studied at the Montréal Museum of Fine Arts and is a graduate of McGill and Yale Universities. A native of Montréal, he has lived and worked in Paris and New York. He presently resides in Montréal.

He is best known for a series of large-scale installations, such as *Les maisons de la rue Sherbrooke,* Montréal (1976), and *A Chicago Construction* (1982), and for the creation of the Canadian Centre for Architecture Garden, Montréal (1987–91), works that have all been widely acclaimed. He is also well known for his photo works, such as *UN DICTIONNAIRE...* (1970–2001), and his photo-based paintings. He has executed major commissions for public sculpture and has won a number of competitions, including the Canadian Tribute to Human Rights, Ottawa, inaugurated in 1991, which has become an important focal point of the nation's capital; a competition for a large-scale installation commissioned by the City of Montréal on the occasion of its 350th anniversary, completed in 1992; and the Canadian Centre for Architecture Garden. In 2004 he executed a major commission for the Ville de Sherbrooke, Québec, a project that comprises an Esplanade, a square (the Place des Moulins), and a large-scale, integrated sculpture that marks the historic center of the town.

Charney's work has been exhibited extensively in Canada and throughout the world, and he has been the subject of retrospective exhibitions at the Art Gallery of Ontario, Toronto (1978); the Musée d'art contemporain de Montréal (1979 and 2002); the Museum of Contemporary Art, Chicago (1982); the Canadian Centre for Architecture, Montréal (1991); the Israel Museum, Jerusalem (1994–95); the Fondation pour l'architecture, Brussels (1994); and Frac Basse-Normandie, Caen (1998). The artist's work has also been included in many group exhibitions, including *An Invitational Exhibition of Contemporary Painting,* Seoul National Museum of Contemporary Art (1990); *La Ville: Art & Architecture en Europe 1870–1993* at the Musée nationale d'art moderne, Centre Georges Pompidou, Paris; *After Auschwitz: Responses to the Holocaust in Contemporary Art* (1995–96), which travelled throughout Great Britain and Germany; *Déclics. Art & Société, le Québec des années 1960 et 1970* at the Musée d'art contemporain de

   Melvin Charney visiting the exhibition *Between Observation and Intervention: The Painted Photographs of Melvin Charney,* Americas Society. Photo: Arturo Sanchez.

Montréal and the Musée de la Civilisation, Québec (1999); *Utopia: The Search for the Ideal Society in the Western World*, Bibliothèque nationale de France, Paris (2001); *Sans commune measure: Image et texte dans l'art actuel*, Centre national de la photographie, Paris (2002); and *Against Architecture: The urgency to (re)think the city*, Espai d'Art Contemporani de Castelló, Valencia (2002). Other notable appearances of his work include those at the Musée d'art moderne de la ville de Paris; P.S.1 Contemporary Art Center, New York; the Kunstverein, Stuttgart; the Akademie der Kunst, Berlin; the National Gallery of Canada, Ottawa; the Musée du Québec, Québec City; the Vancouver Art Gallery; and the Museum of Fine Arts, Montréal. In addition, his work is represented in many permanent collections, both public and private.

Charney's work was included in the Triennale di Milano (1973 and 1985); the Biennale de Paris (1980); and the *Idee, Prozess, Ergebnis, IBAU* exhibition, Berlin (1987). He was invited to participate in Documenta 7 Kassel (1982) and represented Canada twice at the Biennale di Venezia: at the 42nd International Exhibition of Art (1986) and the 7th International Exhibition of Architecture (2000). He has shown with John Weber Gallery, Max Protetch Gallery, Marlborough-Chelsea Gallery, and Frederieke Taylor Gallery, New York; Richard Gray Gallery, Chicago; Galerie C.S. de Beyrie, Paris; Sable-Castelli Gallery, Toronto; and Galerie René Blouin, Montréal. He is currently represented by Nicholas Metivier Gallery, Toronto.

Charney has written and lectured extensively on his work and has been a visiting critic at many universities, including Harvard, Princeton, Columbia, Rice, and The University of California at Berkeley; the University of Melbourne; University College London; and the École nationale supérieure des beaux-arts, Paris.

Monographs devoted to the artist include *Parables and Other Allegories: The work of Melvin Charney, 1975–1991* (1991); *Melvin Charney: Parcours de la réinvention/About Reinvention* (1998); *TRACKING IMAGES: Melvin Charney, UN DICTIONNAIRE…* (2000), published on the occasion of his representing Canada at the 7th Venice Biennale International Exhibition of Architecture; and *Melvin Charney*, published to accompany his retrospective exhibition at the Musée d'art contemporain de Montréal in 2002. Charney's work has been the subject of critical analysis in and has been included in such scholarly texts as *Experimentelle Architekten der Gegenwart* (1991) and *Escape from the Gallery: Deconstructed Art in the Landscape* (1995). Charney has received widespread attention from the international press, with articles and essays about his work appearing in *Artforum, Art in America, Architecture,* and *Perspecta: The Yale Architectural Journal* in the United States; *Domus, d'Architettura,* and *Metamorfosi* in Italy; *Process Architecture* and *S/D* in Japan; *Art Press, Galerie Magazine, Beaux Arts,* and *Archi-Crée* in France; *Contemporary Art, Architectural Design, Design,* and *Architectural Review* in England; and *Espace, C.V., Parachute,* and *Canadian Art* in Canada.

Melvin Charney has been recognized by the Canada Arts Council with several prestigious awards, among them the Lynch-Stanton Award for distinguished artists (1997), and he has been the recipient of the Berliner Künstler Programme, Deutscher Akademischer Austauschdienst (DAAD) award (1982) and the Prix du Québec, Paul-Emile Borduas in the visual arts (1996). In 2003 he was appointed Chevalier dans l'Ordre national du Québec for his outstanding artistic accomplishments and his contribution to the cultural and artistic growth of Québec. In March 2006 he was named Commandeur dans l'Ordre des Arts et des Lettres, the highest honor bestowed by the French government for individual contributions to culture. In 2009 Melvin Charney received a Doctor of Letters, *honoris causa*, from the Faculty of Arts and Faculty of Religious Studies, McGill University.

About the Authors

Gwendolyn Owens

Gwendolyn Owens is a curator and critic who writes on North American art and architecture. Former curator of the Herbert F. Johnson Museum of Art, Cornell University, Ithaca, and former director of The Art Gallery, University of Maryland, College Park, she has been associated with the Canadian Centre for Architecture, Montréal, since 1991; she now serves as the consultant curator of the Gordon Matta-Clark Archive at CCA. Owens's many publications include essays and exhibition catalogues on nineteenth-century American landscape painting; the establishment of a market for American art at the beginning of the twentieth century; and the intersection of art and architectural theory. Her most recent publications include an essay in *Gordon Matta-Clark: "You are the Measure,"* edited by Elisabeth Sussman (Yale University Press, 2007), and a history of the contemporary art center Maryland Art Place (MAP, 2006).

Saul Ostrow

Saul Ostrow is an artist, critic, curator, and editor. He received his M.F.A. from the University of Massachusetts and his B.F.A. from the School of Visual Arts, New York University. Ostrow has served as Dean of the Visual Arts and Technologies program at The Cleveland Institute of Art since 2003, where he is also the Chair of the Visual Arts and Technologies Environment, as well as Department Chair and Associate Professor in Painting. Ostrow has taught at Pratt Institute, Syracuse University, The School of the Visual Arts, New York University, and The University of Connecticut.

Yasmeen Siddiqui

Yasmeen Siddiqui began work at Storefront for Art and Architecture in August 2005 after having completed an M.A. at the Center for Curatorial Studies, Bard College. She is currently an Andy Warhol Foundation Curatorial Research Fellow with a focus on the Futurists and their legacy in architecture and the visual arts. Previously, Siddiqui worked primarily as an art and architecture writer and editor. Selected writings include: "Intimating Architecture" in *Modern Painters* (July–August 2007); "Histories of Violence" in *The Brooklyn Rail* (March 2006); "Nadim Kufi at Gallery 108" in *Flash Art* (2003); and "Emergent Forms: Sabah Naim Reconceptualises Movement" in *Fault Lines, Contemporary African Art and Shifting Landscapes* (Iniva, 2003). From 1999 to 2001 she was senior editor of the Cairo-based architecture magazine *Medina*, and from 2002 to 2004 she edited the MIT online project *ArchNet*.

Selected Bibliography

BOOKS

Chevrier, Jean-François *et al.*: *Melvin Charney: Parcours de la réinvention / About Reinvention* (Caen: Frac Basse-Normandie, 1998).

Landry, Pierre *et al.*: *Melvin Charney* (Montréal: Musée d'art contemporain de Montréal, 2002).

Latour, Alexandra *et al.*: *Parables and Other Allegories: The Work of Melvin Charney, 1975–1990* (Montréal: The Canadian Centre for Architecture, and Cambridge and London: The MIT Press, 1991).

MONOGRAPHS

Dompierre, Louise: *Melvin Charney, 1981–1983* (Kingston: Agnes Etherington Art Centre, Queen's University, 1983).

Lambert, Phyllis *et al.*: *TRACKING IMAGES. Melvin Charney: UN DICTIONNAIRE...* (Montréal: The Canadian Centre for Architecture, 2000).

Tzonis, Alexander: *Melvin Charney, 1970–1979* (Montréal: Musée d'art contemporain de Montréal, 1979).

EXHIBITION CATALOGUES

Bohm-Duchen, Monica *et al.*: *After Auschwitz: Responses to the Holocaust in Contemporary Art* (Sunderland: Northern Centre for Contemporary Art, and London: Lund Humphries, 1995).

Dery, Louise: *Un archipel de désirs: les artistes du Québec et la scène internationale* (Montréal: Musée national des beaux-arts du Québec, 1991).

Dethier, Jean and Alain Guiheux: *La Ville: Art et Architecture en Europe, 1870–1993* (Paris: Éditions du Centre George Pompidou, 1994).

Durand, Régis *et al.*: *Sans commune mesure: image et texte dans l'art actuel* (Paris: Éditions Léo Sheer, 2002).

Gaon, Issike: *dis/PLACEMENTS, The Work of Melvin Charney* (Jerusalem: The Israel Museum, 1996).

Jacobs, Mary-Jane: *Melvin Charney* (Chicago: Museum of Contemporary Art, 1982).

Lamoureux, Johanne: "Melvin Charney: De la construction ou la traduction dès modèles," in *L'art insituable, Collection LIEUdit* (Montréal: Centre de diffusion, 2001).

Lippard, Lucy: "The Inside Picture from the Outside," in *Architectural Sculpture* (Los Angeles: Los Angeles Institute for Contemporary Art, 1980).

Monk, Philip: *Dictionnaire, Parables, In Flight* (Toronto: The Power Plant Gallery of Contemporary Art, 1995).

Nemiroff, Diana: *Canada XLII Biennale di Venezia 1986: Melvin Charney/Krzysztof Wodiczko* (Ottawa: The National Gallery of Canada, 1986).

Oechslin, Werner: *Festarchitectur* (Stuttgart: Akademie der Archiektenkammer Nordhein-Westfalen and Verlag Gerd Hatje, 1984).

Pagé, Suzanne: "Melvin Charney: Quelques Monuments Nationaux," in *Canada Trajectoires—'73* (Paris: A.R.C., Musée d'Art moderne de la ville de Paris, 1973).

Pontbriand, Chantal: "Melvin Charney: l'in situ en mémoire," in *Fragments Critiques, 1978–1998* (Paris: Éditions Jacqueline Chambord, 1998).

Townsend-Gault, Charlotte: "Wavelength to Paternity: Epistemology with a Camera," in *Frame of Mind: Viewpoints on Photography in Contemporary Canadian Art* (Banff: Walter Phillips Gallery, 1993).

REVIEWS, COMMENTARIES, PROFILES

Bagg, Shannon: "Melvin Charney and the Temple of Jerusalem," *Journal of the Society for the Study of Architecture in Canada*, Vol.24, No.2 (Ottawa: 1999).

Battisti, Eugenio: "Contro l'International Style," *Casa del Libro* (January 1982).

Bedard, Catherine: "Melvin Charney," *Parachute*, No.61 (January–March 1991).

Béret, Chantal: "Biennale de Venise, du bien et du beau, ni plus, ni moins—Ethically Correct in Venice," *Artpress*, No.260 (September 2000).

Burkhardt, Lucius: "Melvin Charney," *Werk und Zeit*, No.4 (April 1981).

Charre, Alain: "Melvin Charney: Pour une culture du regard," *VISUEL(S) revue d'arts*, No.7/8 (Fall 1999).

Chaslin, François: "Architectes en désir des arts," *Les cahiers du musée d'art moderne, Centre Georges Pompidou*, No.39 (Spring 1992).

Chevrier, Jean-François: "La discipline et l'art du document: Melvin Charney, UN DICTIONNAIRE...," *Cahiers thématiques: architecture, histoire, conception, École d'architecture de Lille* (February 2001).

Chevrier, Jean-François: "Melvin Charney," *Galeries Magazine*, No.58 (February–March 1994).

Cohen, Ronny H.: "Citysite Sculpture Visual Arts Ontario," *Artforum*, Vol.21, No.5 (January 1982).

Dault, Gary Michael: "Layers of endless possibilities," *The Globe and Mail* (December 6, 2003).

Dery, Louise: "Charney: le pouvoir de transfiguration," *ARQ Architecture/Québec*, No.65 (February 1992).

Durand, Régis: "Photographies canadiennes contemporaines," *Artpress*, No.186 (December 1993).

Forgey, Benjamin: "Reflections in a City Garden: The Canadian Centre of Architecture, Apple of Montreal's Eye," *The Washington Post* (September 22, 1990).

Forster, Kurt W.: "Contradictions of Preservation and Destruction," *Architext* (December 1983).

Fulford, Robert: "Icons and Allegories: The Sculpture Garden of Melvin Charney," *Canadian Art*, Vol.8, No.1 (Spring 1991).

Goddard, Peter: "Melvin Charney. The master art builder," *Toronto Star* (October 18, 2003).

Hutchison, Bill: "To build a house in Paradise," *The Whig-Standard Magazine* (March 16, 1983).

Lamoureux, Johanne: "Melvin Charney, l'architecture mise en jeu," *Artpress*, No.123 (March 1988).

Lehmann, Henry: "The city re-imagined," *The Gazette* (March 22, 2008).

McConathy, Dale: "Corridart: Instant Archeology in Montreal," *Artscanada*, No.206/207 (July–August 1976).

McDougall, Ian and Cathy Peake: "Melvin Charney," *Transition*, Vol.2, No.2 (June 1981).

Millet, Catherine: "Melvin Charney: explorateur de la mémoire collective: Interview par Catherine Millet," *Artpress*, No.202 (May 1995)

Milroy, Sarah: "An Urban Artist's Building Blocks," *The Globe and Mail* (April 20, 2002).

Morgan, Ann Lee: "A Chicago Letter," *Art International*, Vol.9–10, (November–December 1982).

Needham, Gerald: "Melvin Charney: Constructs and Concepts," *Artscanada*, No.234/235 (April–May 1980).

Östling, Johan: "Prolog," in *Nazismens sens-moral* (Stockholm: Atlantis Press, 2008).

Restany, Pierre: "Melvin Charney: Giardino-sculture del CCA a Montreal," *Domus*, No.712 (January 1990).

Russell, John: "Art: Where to See the New Work," *The New York Times* (June 8, 1979).

Teshigawara, Jan: "Melvin Charney," in *Escape from the Gallery: Deconstructed Art in the Landscape* (Tokyo: Gendaikikakushitsu Publishers, 1995).

Thomsen, Christian W.: "Melvin Charney: Practizierte Architektur-philosophien," in *Experimentelle Architekten der Gegenwart* (Cologne: DuMont Buchverlag, 1991).

Tiberghien, Gilles A.: "Notes 3," in *Notes sur la nature...* (Paris: Éditions du Félin, 2005).

Vastel, Michel: "Sherbrooke se jette à l'eau," *L'actualité* (March 15–18, 2005).

Vernes, Michel: "Paysages d'ici et d'ailleurs: sur l'architecture outre mesure de Melvin Charney," *ARCHI-CREE*, No.248 (June–July 1992).

Zevi, Bruno: "Projetto canadese per Osaka '70," *L'Architettura*, Vol.13, No.8 (December 1967).

Acknowledgments

Numerous individuals and institutions have contributed to making this exhibition and publication a reality. We wish especially to thank Melvin Charney for his advice and for generously giving of his time, spent attending to the many tasks associated with the organization of the exhibition and accompanying book. Guest curator Gwendolyn Owens dedicated countless hours in this project, which are reflected in both the exhibition and the publication. We are extremely grateful to the authors who contributed to the understanding of Melvin Charney's work and to Isabela Villanueva for her patience coordinating this volume.

The successful implementation of this project has been possible thanks to the joint efforts of the Musée national des beaux-arts du Québec. We are indebted to their staff for their invaluable support.

For assistance with the research and organization of the exhibition, we would also like to thank Cécile Baird, Fabienne Bilodeau, Lisa Davie, Edward Dimendberg, Phyllis Lambert, Pierre Landry, Alessandra LaTour, Réjean Legault, Robin Mader, Michel Martin, Marc Mayer, Line Ouellet, Ross J.Q. Owens, and Cecil Rabinovitch.

We would like to give special mention to Carlos Brillembourg, Dan Graham, Susan Herrington, Anthony Kiendl, Saul Ostrow, and Yasmeen Siddiqui for their valuable contributions to the public programs that accompanied the exhibition. Storefront for Art and Architecture and its director, Joseph Grima, partnered with Americas Society in an insightful panel discussion that provided the opportunity to discuss Melvin Charney's work in a broader context.

This major undertaking was made possible through the generous support of individuals and institutions from the United States and Canada. Americas Society gratefully acknowledges the following friends, colleagues, and collectors for allowing us to borrow works of art: National Gallery of Canada, Ottawa; Musée des Beaux-Arts de Montréal; Caisse de depot et placement du Québec; Gordon Ridgely Collection; Richard Cooper Collection; Jared Sable Collection, Toronto; Ruth and Sam Karpman Collection; Amesbury Chalmers Collection; Norman Damiani and Hélène Barabé Collection; Melvin Charney Collection; Rosamond Ivey Collection, Toronto; Bella and Irving Borwick Collection; and many private collectors.